d Redemption
Church, P ogy in Ireland

Terence P. McCaughey

MEMORY AND REDEMPTION

Church, Politics and Prophetic Theology in Ireland

Gill & Macmillan

Published in Ireland by
Gill & Macmillan Ltd
Goldenbridge
Dublin 8
with associated companies throughout the world

0 7171 2094 5

Index compiled by Helen Litton
Print origination by
Seton Music Graphics Ltd, Bantry, Co. Cork
Printed by Colour Books Ltd, Dublin

A catalogue record is available for this book from the British Library.

Note on cover design:

The drawing on the front cover is based on an illustration in a medallion at the base of Chi Ro page of the *Book of Kells*. It represents cats and rats playing together. In the centre two rats are holding up or eating what appears to be the Host. In this domestic treatment of Isaiah's version of the day when the 'lion will lie down with the lamb', the hostility between the two mutually incompatible species is apparently to be transcended by another reality.

Oblivion is at the root of exile, the way memory is at the root of redemption.

BAAL SHEM TOV

Then I saw in my Dream, that the Shepherds had them to another place, in a bottom, where was a door in the side of an Hill; and they opened the door, and bid them look in. They looked in, therefore, and saw that within it was very dark and smoky; they also thought that they heard there a rumbling noise as of Fire, and a cry of some tormented, and that they smelt the scent of Brimstone. Then said Christian, what means this? The shepherds told them, saying, this is a By-way to Hell, a way that Hypocrites go in at; namely, such as sell their Birthright, with Esau; such as sell their Master, with Judas; such as blaspheme the Gospel, with Alexander, and that lie and dissemble, with Ananias and Sapphira his wife.

Then said Hopeful to the Shepherds, I perceive that these had on them, even every one, a shew of Pilgrimage, as we have now; had they not?

Shep. Yes, and held it a long time too.
Hope. How far might they go on in Pilgrimage in their day, since they notwithstanding were thus miserably cast away?
Shep. Some farther, and some not so far as these Mountains.
Then said the Pilgrims one to another, We had need cry to the Strong for strength.
Shep. Ay, and you will have need to use it when you have it too.

By this time the Pilgrims had a desire to go forwards and the Shepherds a desire they should; so they walked together towards the end of the Mountains. Then said the Shepherds one to another, Let us here shew to the Pilgrims the Gates of the Coelestial City, if they have skill to look through our Perspective Glass. The Pilgrims then lovingly accepted the motion; so they had them to the top of an high Hill, called Clear, and gave them their Glass to look. Then they essayed to look, but the remembrance of that last thing that the shepherds had shewed them made their hands shake, by means of which impediment they could not look steadily through the Glass; yet they thought they saw something like the Gate, and also some of the Glory of the place.

John Bunyan, THE PILGRIM'S PROGRESS

Contents

ACKNOWLEDGMENTS

Since the current 'troubles' began in 1968, a good deal of discussion has taken place as to whether or not the problem in the north of Ireland could be described as a religious one, or is better described in economic and political terms. Much of this particular discussion has reached the printed page. The Irish political and cultural situation has no doubt also generated a good deal of theological reflection—much of it of a high quality. This book is written in the hope that it may provoke people who have not done so to commit their theological perceptions and reflections on our condition to paper. I am very grateful to Professor Seán Freyne who encouraged me to write in the first place, and who patiently read through the first draft, making many valuable suggestions as to how it could be improved. I acknowledge in particular the debt we all owe to Professor Enda MacDonagh for the contributions he has made in this field and the way in which conversations with him have contributed to anything that is worthwhile in this book.

I would also gratefully acknowledge the support and help I have received from colleagues in Trinity College, Dublin: Dr Gabriel Daly, Dr Werner Jeanrond, Professor Andrew Mayes. Many others not specifically mentioned here will recognise the impact of what they have said on what I have written. I hope they will not be impatient with the use I have made of their insights and will accept my thanks.

My thanks are especially due to Aedín Ní Earchaí for the patience and skill with which she produced an acceptable typescript of the first draft, and to Alison Finlay for all her work on the second.

Lastly, I would like to thank my wife and family for allowing me time which was really theirs to get this written.

Pentecost 1992 — Terence P. McCaughey

Introduction

Over the past twenty years or more, the Churches in Ireland have come under both internal and external pressure to 'speak out' on the political situation. Politicians, recognising that the conflict in the North had at least some sort of religious dimension, have sought to enlist the support of Churches in this or that policy of their own and have encouraged Church leadership to give a lead to what is called 'their people'. This has promoted a tendency which was already there, for the Churches to adopt the role of spokespersons or representatives of one of the two sides in a divided community.

But it is only fair to say that this one-sided role has not been felt to be adequate by everyone. There has survived in each of the Churches a number of people who recognise that 'speaking out' must involve more than simply articulating the hopes and fears of one's 'own people'. From within the ranks of Church members themselves there has been heard a persistent call for the articulation of a more comprehensive comment on our predicament. The most instructed may even use the terms 'prophetic witness' or 'prophetic voice' to describe this comment. In doing so, they are making a wholly reasonable request, for the Church is after all a community that has over centuries hailed Christ not only as priest and as king, but also as prophet, and has claimed that Christ's Church shares with Christ in all three of these roles. But, that being said, what does a 'prophetic witness' mean in practice? Is it any more than a Church-y way of saying that we expect representative Christians to speak out clearly and courageously? Or is there a recognition here of a precise function, rooted in the Judaeo-Christian tradition, which can still be exercised by the believing community, even in modern Ireland.

Both Jews and Christians recognise in their scriptures material by and about persons who are termed *prophets*; it is no doubt to this material and these traditions that people are appealing when they call for a 'prophetic witness'. But the prophets are not the only group whose voice can be heard in the tradition. Two other groups are discernible, i.e. the *sages* and the *priests.* The vision of reality cherished by each of these two groups was centered respectively on the study of Torah and on the divine worship in the Jerusalem temple. Each of these visions is of primary importance; and it must be conceded that at any time in Israel's history ordinary people lived more or less simultaneously within all three of them. Certainly, if we listen to the voice of only *one* of these groups, to the exclusion of the other two, we curtail quite drastically our chances of understanding how Israel understood itself. This book, by selecting the prophetic tradition for special consideration, does not intend to undervalue that of the 'priests' or the 'sages'. It starts out from a recognition of the fact that the prophets trained their sights on matters which were of little concern to the sages and the priests. Nevertheless these are the very matters which in the very different historical circumstances of our time, concern us in Ireland today as we seek to formulate a response to our predicament.

But first, let us look back into the life of Israel to discern what those concerns were. Jacob Neusner notes that the priestly class, who were in charge of the temple, had been energetic and wily in negotiating a secure position for the temple and the cult under the general aegis of the Roman Empire. The priests saw everything in terms of that temple and that cult. 'To the priest', says Neusner, 'the sacred society of Israel produced no history except for what happened *in* the temple and *to* the temple . . . All lands outside the land of Israel were chronically unclean . . . From such a perspective on the world, no doctrine of Israel among the nations, no interest in the history of Israel and in the meaning of its past and future were apt to emerge.'[1]

The sage, on the other hand, was concerned primarily with what happened in the home and the market-place from day to day. For the sage, life in those spheres was seen as governed by rules which could be deduced from the revealed law of God in Torah. The wisdom of the sage was firmly based in interpretation, on interpretation of the text of Torah itself and also on explication of what earlier interpreters of it had said. This wisdom could be thought of as having universal application insofar as it dealt with relationships which, in varying forms, reappear at all times and in all societies, i.e. as between fathers and sons, servants and employers, teachers and disciples. Significantly, however, the sages were not concerned with 'nations, armies and destiny'.

But precisely these things had always been the concern of the prophets. In Jesus' day, the line of prophets is understood to have petered out. But it can be said that those in his day who looked for the coming of the Messiah who would liberate Israel so that she could fulfil her international destiny, stood in succession to the prophets of an earlier time. Of such a kind was for instance John the Baptiser. Speaking of the prophets, Neusner notes that they insisted that the fate of the nation depended upon its faith and moral condition.

The cult, of which the priestly class were guardians, existed in order to ensure the continuity of the nation's life in harmony with God and God's creation: it was therefore by definition timeless. The wisdom of the sages and rabbis was deemed to be of universal application: it was therefore also timeless. Again as Neusner puts it: 'Both sage and priest saw Israel from the aspect of eternity. But the nation lived out its life in this world, among other people coveting the very same land, within the politics of empire.' It is to this context in universal terms and to the fabric of social morality in national terms, that the prophets addressed themselves untiringly. These concerns are *not* timeless; they are essentially historical. The prophets subjected the sacred national history which was tirelessly celebrated in the cult, to a critical gaze. That is why we begin the first chapter of this book with a look, not alone at the stories which we in Ireland tell about ourselves, but also at the way we celebrate and re-enact the stories to influence the present and even to ensure a particular kind of future, insofar as that is envisioned. We take a look at what may be termed our sacred national histories.

In Ireland we could claim that we have had an equivalent to the priestly-cultic tradition too, both prior to the period of the Protestant Reformation and since. Churches, endowed with what Troeltsch called 'the objective treasures of grace and redemption', have attempted to keep their people in touch with a timeless reality.[2] This has been specially valuable at times when the realities of people's lives in time and place became almost unbearable. In the exercise of their function, the Irish ecclesiastical leadership has been every bit as wily as the Sadducees of Jesus' time in their efforts to ensure the security and continuity of the cult and its prestige as the national religion. As institutions, however, the Churches have sought to avoid hard questions concerning 'nations, armies and destiny', even though they were prepared, when called upon, to bless the arms of combatants or anathematise the enemy. Equally certainly we can lay claim to a tradition in a measure equivalent to that of the sages of Israel, a tradition of meditation on the received wisdom concerning the spectrum of relationships in school and market-place or in the family or the home.

It would be churlish to deny the value of either of these. But equally it would be a mistake not to recognise that it is primarily upon the prophetic tradition of Israel and early Christianity that we should draw if we are to respond to the call to 'speak out'. Of course, it must be conceded that the prophetic tradition is not the only one represented in the Hebrew Bible or the Christian scripture. In the New Testament itself it would appear that, for instance, Jesus of Nazareth and Paul stand within that tradition in a way that John does not. In the chapters which follow we use the biblical material selectively, while acknowledging that the very existence of priestly or wisdom literature in the Bible serves as a reminder that the prophetic tradition cannot survive on its own for long. It requires also the values and the vision represented by the sage and the priest. It was, after all, in the temple precincts at the hour of prayer that Isaiah received his call to be a prophet. It was in the same place that Jeremiah came to an enriched understanding of just what implications for social life must be drawn by conscientious worshippers.[3]

Students of religion have for a long time distinguished two types of prophecy or divination:

(1) *inductive or instrumental divination*, and (2) *intuitive or mediated divination.* The first of these involves the interpretation of signs and omens. Among Israel's neighbours, it was the Assyrians and Babylonians in particular who developed the 'reading' of omens into a kind of science. Inductive divination of this sort does not occupy a very important place in the Hebrew Bible, but one form of it is mentioned somewhat dismissively in the following saying of Jesus:

> When you see a cloud rising in the west, you say at once, 'A shower is coming'; and so it happens. And when you see the south wind blowing, you say, 'There will be scorching heat'; and it happens. You hypocrites! You know how to interpret the appearance of earth and sky; but why do you not know how to interpret the present time? [4]

What he is commending to his hearers is a sensitive attention to the 'omens' in *human history and experience*, a discerning of the times, such as the prophets of Israel had constantly engaged in. As they looked at the social, religious or economic life of the people, the prophets recognised what they believed to be the inevitable consequences. As Klaus Koch puts it:

> It is their stress of the underlying meaning of the present which gives the prophets' ideas their splendour—and also their limitation.[5]

The opening chapters of this book are an endeavour to follow the prophets' example in this respect by examining the underlying meanings which may be drawn from our varying understandings of the present and the past. Underlying meanings have been discerned and celebrated which could bolster the claims of what is here for convenience termed *Catholic nationalism* and *Protestant unionism.* These understandings and the version of history re-enacted to support them have to be examined before we can re-tell the story of the Irish people in a more comprehensive way with enlarged understanding and extended perspective. In the time of Amos the people still thought of themselves as an elect people monopolising the love and providence of God. Amos explodes this exclusivism in an oracle in which he concludes that God has a purpose for the neighbouring peoples other than simply their defeat or their destruction. Amos's vision amplifies and expands two things: (a) his understanding of God and (b) his understanding of the demands and responsibilities which such a God lays upon the people. He takes the story of Israel, as commonly repeated, and sets it in an enlarged context which now includes the Philistines and the poor of Israel itself.[6]

The second mode of divination is the *intuitive.* According to this, the human medium passes on a message received by some sort of divine inspiration. The heading to the oracles of Isaiah reads, 'the *vision* of Isaiah, which he *saw*'; it indicates that what we are about to read is something other than conclusions drawn from empirical analysis. Koch sums up the process thus:

> The normal Israelite is incapable of meeting with what the prophet undergoes as private experience, but he is able to enter into it through a subsequent process of perception, and to accept it as true. The prophets do not aim to proclaim a mystery which could only be accepted by surrendering reason. But they do take to task the foolish people who do not trust God's inspiration and do not permit themselves to be moved to subsequent insight.[7]

This is something different from the inductive divination we have spoken of, but it is equally characteristic of the prophets. Their vision is peculiar to themselves but their revelation for the future never loses touch with present conditions. In fact, it *illuminates* them, and it is normally to be implemented by human, not divine or semi-divine agents. That is why their oracles can so often be read as a kind of invitation to follow up the inspiration and 'to verify, in a process of subsequent insight, what seems to have been revealed to them by the divine forerunner.'[8]

The prophets are seen again as straining towards and yearning for a moral world order and a future of enhanced human dignity. Wholly consistent with this is their preoccupation with the appointment and the deposition of kings. To the same Saul the prophet Samuel says at one time, 'The Lord has anointed you to be prince over his heritage' and, a few years later, 'The Lord has torn the kingdom of Israel from you this day, and given it to a neighbour of yours, who is better than you.' (1 Sam. 10.1; 15.28). For two hundred years in the northern kingdom the prophets fomented revolution, at the rate of roughly one every fifty years. But, even in the southern kingdom where the successors of David were hailed at inauguration with the title 'Son of God', the kings were servants not descendants of the deity, *anointed* by God not *descended* from God. Nathan, a court prophet who is sufficiently well placed to intrigue on behalf of Solomon as his father David's successor, nevertheless, at an earlier stage, entered the palace to reproach David for his adultery with Bathsheba and the murder of her husband, and to pronounce the judgment of God on the king for what he had done.[9]

In the end, after centuries of endeavour, it appears as though the prophets came to the conclusion that it was impossible to give political expression to the notion of a people at one with Yahweh, their God. They had wanted the kingdom of God in Israel here and now. Frustrated in that, they were driven to the extremity of conceiving the possibility that God could and would even order their deportation from the land of Israel and bring about the downfall of monarchy and state. It became possible even to see the heathen King Cyrus of Babylon as *God's* instrument. In the expectation of *universal* change, they began to develop an outlook which we might even call *eschatological.* God's kingship came to be thought of as belonging to the future, a future which gives shape and meaning to our fragmentary present. By the time prophecy gave way to apocalyptic, the context of thought had been immeasurably widened. What it was going to mean to salute Yahweh as 'king' was extended beyond any previous understanding.

It is altogether appropriate to see Christian faith as the ultimate in that process of context-widening to which prophets bear witness. Paul and the Hellenistic mission to which he belonged, seem to have understood their faith in such a light. They appear to have discerned in the events around Jesus of Nazareth the breaking-down of the last barriers that separate. For them the good news of the gospel was precisely that God was now calling all people everywhere, not through the imperium of Rome or by adherence to the law of Moses, but through Jesus of Nazareth, put to death under both of these. The early Church's proclamation of Jesus as raised from the dead is itself an affirmation of belief in a future which radically questions and transcends the ideologies of Jerusalem and Rome—indeed, ideology of any kind. Insofar as we aspire to stand in that succession, our task in Ireland today lies in re-assessing our ideologies by 'verifying, in a process of subsequent insight, what seems to have been revealed to us by the divine forerunner.'

The prophets in their day, as they contemplated repeated political failures to establish the kingship of Yahweh in Israel, were driven towards an eschatological perspective. And so are we, if we are prepared to look our two dominant Irish ideologies in the eye. In chapter 10 we will consider the extent to which God's longed-for yet sometimes feared future becomes or should become the catalyst of Christian reflection and action. Of course, it is true that the Churches in Ireland have been apt to do violence to the possibility of this actually happening, in that their established position has inclined them to represent the faith as primarily concerned for the preservation of a tradition, and for little else.

Whenever the Church becomes secure in society it quite understandably tends to take that line. As a valued part of the establishment, Christians have tended to lose any acute sense of being 'sojourners or aliens in a strange land'. Nevertheless, from time to time, that idea has re-emerged, as has the primitive sense of belonging to a 'commonwealth' (*politeuma*) that already exists, and is even already present in our society *in nuce*, challenging it in one way or another. Wherever this insight was recovered, the Christian task in the social and political field was once again seen to be nothing other than the endeavour to discern what contours this incipient *politeuma* may or must necessarily have as it enters particular communities and cultures.

Of course, the Christian community itself has taken more varied forms than it would be possible here to rehearse or to describe. But there is value in referring to the two-fold categorisation of Ernst Troeltsch i.e. the distinction between 'Church' and 'sect'. This distinction is valuable, not least for the fact that 'Churches' and 'sects' have two clearly distinguishable perceptions as to how exactly the kingdom is realised in human society. According to Troeltsch's view, 'the Church is an institution endowed with grace and salvation . . . able to receive the masses and to adjust itself to the world, because to a certain extent, it can afford to ignore the need for subjective holiness for the sake of the objective treasures of grace and redemption.' The sect, on the other hand, is a 'voluntary society' bound together by some sense of a 'new birth' in common. They live largely 'apart from the world' and live in preparation for the *coming* kingdom of God. 'Churches' according to this definition, attempt to permeate the society at large by such means as are at any particular time available to them. On the other hand, wherever Christians gather in a 'sect', they tend to anathematise society at large. But sometimes, as in the case of the Catholic religious orders or Protestant communities like the Moravians, they have aimed rather to be a sign to the State or to the mass of believers of an alternative way of life. They may regard the kingdom, in which all wrongs will be righted, as either coming in a remote or in a very immediate future. These two forms of Christian social organisation represent clearly divergent understandings of how exactly the values of the kingdom are realised in human society. It would probably be true to say that most Irish Christians have been reared in a 'Church', rather than a 'sect' setting.[10]

From time to time, of course, communities of either type have lost their eschatological perspective. Where this has happened it has usually had disastrous results, in that they have then collapsed community and kingdom into one another. But wherever the believing community has been true to its calling, it has not held any ultimate hope for itself other than that finally it would be the 'bride of Christ', i.e. be made one with him. On the way to that consummation its task was understood to be the facilitation of the emergent new Jerusalem, the real heavenly State. For, in the primitive Christian understanding, it is worth remembering that it is the State not the Church, which constitutes the 'new age'. Cf. Revelation 21 which speaks of a new community and State, but not of a new temple.

Christians, insofar as they announce the kingdom and the consequently provisional character of all ideology, religious or political, share in Christ's prophetic office. This they are called upon to do dramatically from time to time, as in Hitler's Germany, in South Africa and elsewhere. But often their most significant contribution is painstakingly to work out, with others in the political arena, the implications of what they recognise as Christ's lordship and that incipient reality which Jesus spoke of as the 'kingdom of God' and which, by word and deed, he anticipated. This contribution is made within a process which Klaus Koch calls 'subsequent insight', but which the New Testament refers to as the work of 'conscience'. The Western tradition has, of course, tended to individualise and privatise conscience and its operation in a way that is hard to substantiate by reference to the New Testament. For in the New Testament: (1) the word translated 'conscience' really means something more like *consciousness*; (2) it refers to a collective as much as to an individual phenomenon; and (3) it refers to consciousness not alone of empirically verifiable reality but also of an imminent reality making its way into our present. The development of a shared consciousness of this imminent reality and perception of the social and political possibilities it might realise is very like the 'subsequent insight' which the prophets of Israel hoped to awaken by their oracles. (Chapters 8–10, below).

In the final chapter we turn to the tricky questions posed for Christian commentary and action by the fact that even here in Ireland Christendom is nearly gone. This is not to say that the vestiges and monuments of Christendom are not all around us; for better and for worse they are, and certainly we cannot pretend that that history did not happen. However, we are not free to return to the roles of pre-Constantinian sect or national Church or Holy Roman Empire, even if we wished to. Ironically, those in the Irish Churches who most jealously guard the sacred position of the Church(es) in society are apt in the process to end up by secularising them more surely than any of the secularising forces they fear so much, will ever do. For insistence on the 'position of the Church' serves often merely to reduce it to the status of being no more than the religious factor in a total situation, making its voice heard alongside of other interests—sporting, trade unions, employers' federations, women's groups etc.

If, as Christians or as groups of Christians, we are to operate within the political arena at all, we must not hanker after models from the past, whether of sect or Church. If we are to avoid being as prescriptive as 'Churches' have tended to be, and as dismissive of the views of others as 'sects' have usually been, then we have to seek new and appropriate ways in which to be present in society. In doing so we will probably also wish to salvage from our Christian past what we cannot readily afford to lose, i.e. that comprehensive sense of responsibility for everything which has always characterised the Churches, and the detached stance of the sects with their passion for personal and collective holiness here and now.

1

Winners' and Losers' Stories

Old Norse literature distinguishes between two types of saga—the 'true' and the 'lying'. 'True' sagas tell about the settlement of Iceland and the conflicts and struggles of the founding families. They are understood to be an accurate account of those early days. The 'lying' sagas, on the other hand, were written and read aloud purely for entertainment. They represent a type of story-telling which is to be found in many cultures, i.e. stories that are told just for fun. But in fact, even stories of this sort often turn out to serve a purpose or 'to have a point'. Children's games and rhymes are often the childish repetition of adult rites which, in the course of time, have become the distinguishing rituals of a children's peer group. The *Märchen* collected by the brothers Grimm or the oral tales of the Irish countryside, which we tell our children or read to them at bedtime, once served to reinforce the values and norms of a society. The hero, who is usually male, survives by his wits, is rewarded for his fidelity and honesty and most often ends up getting the hand of the king's daughter in marriage.

The stories celebrated or re-enacted in religious cults are re-enacted because they are believed to tell the truth about some event in the remote past which is deemed to have significance still. Those devotees who hear and/or re-enact the sacred story are considered to be made thereby in some way participant in the timeless drama. What was true in that remote past is deemed still to be true today. The act of re-telling serves in a sense to make time and the world stand still and even to ensure that things will be, now and in the future, as they were in the beginning. So for instance in the Hebrew tradition, the farmer offering the first-fruits of his crop to God, is invited by the writer of Deuteronomy to identify with his ancestor Jacob who went down to Egypt, and with the descendants of Jacob who came out of Egypt at the exodus, rescued by God, and were brought into the very land which now yields them first-fruits which the worshipper presents to God as an offering.[1] The farmer's present claim to the land is confirmed by reference to the ancient story and by identifying the characters in that story with himself. The story he is bidden to recite is itself a triumphant one with a happy outcome. It moves from rags to riches or, at any rate, from starvation to self-sufficiency, and the worshipper identifies with that movement.

Presumably it was easy enough for the Israelite farmer to make that ritual identification with Jacob and the escaping Israelites of Moses' time whose sagas he had often heard repeated. But it is not always so easy for later people to make such identifications. Take the case of the aborigines in Australia in 1988. In that year the Commonwealth and State governments officially celebrated what was popularly called the 'bicentenary' of Australia. Even when this was glossed as the bicentenary of the European settlement of Australia, aborigines had cause to be affronted, and were. Looking round them at what had been done to their best land, their sacred places and their people, they wondered what exactly they were being asked to celebrate. Their own stories do not fit into any calendar, Julian or Gregorian. They do not require chronology. They stretch backward across the fleeting nightmare of the white man's occupancy to the first days and nights of time, present in a great continuum at the sacred trees and waterholes. We may ask how exactly the narratives of the voyages of 'discovery' sound in the ears of those who know that they were there all the time. How were those losers ever expected to participate in the celebration and re-enactment of the winners' story?

The fact is, of course, that the constant repetition and re-enactment of the winners' story tends to create a world in which no other story has currency or value. In Ireland examples of this tendency and its effects abound and are too numerous to cite. One thinks, for instance, of the official visit of the late President Seán T. Ó Ceallaigh to the Vatican, in the course of which the president assured His Holiness of 'the obedience of the Irish people'. It was an understandable turn of phrase but, coming from the president of a State with 5 per cent of Protestants and from an Ireland with something like 25 per cent of Protestants, it was an inexcusable slip. Protestants and others were disappointed, not because it mattered to them what the president said to the Pope in the audience chamber of the Vatican, but because they suddenly saw that in the view of the first citizen of the State the experience and loyalties of the Roman Catholic majority were normative for all. Unfortunately the stories of 'the Irish people' and that of the Catholic people of Ireland were still being collapsed into one another by Pope John Paul II's script-writers when he visited Ireland in 1979. On the other side, one might cite the example of Mr Jim Molyneux and Dr Paisley when they wrote to Mrs Thatcher to protest against the possibility of any agreement coming to be signed which might conceivably give the Irish government a say in the affairs of the North. In exclusivist style they spoke of '*the people of Ulster*' (sic) as being 'profoundly anxious'. A study of Dr Paisley's own usage shows clearly that 'people of Ulster' and 'Protestant people of Ulster' are interchangeable terms. The other inhabitants of Northern Ireland are often referred to simply as 'the enemies of Ulster', of whose story and of whose aspirations the less that is said the better.

Losers everywhere and throughout history have usually been faced with two possibilities. They may either continue to whisper their own story to one another more or less resentfully, or they may simply give up and try to identify with the winners' story and with the triumph and the vision which its re-enactment aims to sustain. Happily, in Ireland and in other parts of the world, losers have seized upon a third possibility. Various kinds of 'losers'—the racially oppressed, the poor, women and others—have taken the opportunity afforded by radio, television and the specialist presses, to make their experience audible and visible to a wider world. This has served to raise their morale, but it has done more. For just as the stories of the dominant group have aimed all along to keep things from changing, so the telling of the stories of the dominated and oppressed may come to subvert the present order and disposition of power.

It has often been observed that in Ireland we have today a political and demographic configuration in which there is a complex of interlocking majorities and minorities. Since 1922 Protestants have been a majority north of the border and a minority south and west of it. Catholics, who form roughly 75 per cent of the total population of Ireland, have been reduced in the North to being no more than one-third of the population, while forming the overwhelming majority in the twenty-six county State. The partition of Ireland had the effect of establishing two political units, both of which accepted in principle the values of the liberal tradition. But both of them had come into existence at least in part as a result of religious confessional divisions. Post-1921, each part of Ireland has had in varying measure the features of a confessional State, and this characteristic did not greatly diminish with the passage of time. Both unionists and nationalists could claim in 1922 to have salvaged something from the conflict. Catholic-nationalists celebrated what had been wrenched from the conqueror's grasp and in their celebration looked forward to the completion of the task. Unionists celebrated the staunch resistance of the Ulster Protestants to Home Rule. In their celebrations they still seek to ensure that what they salvaged for themselves will never be taken away from them.

Each of these groups was now in a majority somewhere. Equally certainly it was also in a minority somewhere else. In the North, where their two ideologies had always confronted one another most fiercely, it was particularly easy to see that what they were seeking was mastery, one over the other. Realistic observers, who are themselves neither intransigent nor irredentist, have always recognised that, in any serious confrontation between the two, one or other must inevitably give way. Where a particular version of history is that of the majority, it serves to maintain the majority's dominance. When a version of history is that of the minority, it serves to modify, challenge or even to subvert the *status quo.* So the significance of a particular story or version of history depends entirely on whether it is on the lips of 'winners' or 'losers'. Recitation of the long story of struggle for Catholic civil rights or emancipation or to the events of Easter week 1916 is quite a different thing in West Belfast or the Bogside from what it is in a comfortable Dublin suburb. It is not merely that the surroundings are different: the function of the recitation is radically different. In the same way, an appeal to the Protestant respect for 'civil and religious liberties', when made in defense of the Adelaide Hospital in Dublin or the right of citizens to divorce or contraception as civil rights, may be considered as rather different from an appeal to the same liberties when made at the end of an Orange walk to the accompaniment of a Lambeg drum.

Over the past decade or so liberals brought up in both these traditions, understandably alarmed by sectarian outrages, have spoken of the need to listen to one another and of the need to respect or even cherish one another's tradition. This has led to an exploration of the possibility of what has been called 'reconciling our memories'.[2] Insofar as this endeavour represents an effort to get people who have not been doing so to listen to one another, it is an advance. Particularly in Belfast, but certainly not only there, it has been possible for people to live out their lives within only one community. Under such circumstances it can only be a good thing for a Protestant to learn what it has been like to grow up in the Catholic ghetto. Even inside what is called 'the Protestant community' itself, it can only be a salutary thing for the middle class Protestant to learn at first hand how it feels to belong to the Protestant *petit bourgeois* or working class, to come to know their fears and their resentments.

But when the winners or the relatively privileged first hear how things appear to the less privileged or the downright oppressed, they are liable to be shocked or frankly incredulous. For, in the story of the poor and the oppressed, they may discover that they and their forebears play the villain's part. And this will inevitably arouse in good and earnest people an unexpectedly poignant sense of guilt. Many unionists have developed a bad conscience of this sort since 1969, even if they did not have it before. A similar development has taken place within the ranks of Catholic nationalism. One does not have to concur with every conclusion which Dr Conor Cruise O'Brien has drawn since, in order to be grateful to him for holding the mirror up to the face of Catholic nationalism, making it see in itself certain unacceptably imperialist pretensions.[3]

Factors which we will be examining in chapters 2 and 3 have co-operated to undermine the self-confidence of the liberally-minded among the ranks of both Protestant-unionists and Catholic-nationalists. What is sometimes called 'revisionist' historiography has knocked away some of their supporting props. The result has been that many reasonably well-educated people, brought up in these traditions, have either come to feel that what they were brought up to believe is a shade unsophisticated, or they have actually developed a very bad conscience indeed about the past altogether—their forebears' past and their own. They have resorted to various stratagems in order to deal with this, as we shall see in chapter 5. One of these strategies has been to try to respect the two traditions equally. It is contended here that this is not a productive policy, since neither of the traditions nor their supportive versions of history are anything more than the popular justification of pretensions to dominance by one group over the other. Insofar as that is the use they have been put to, they cannot be considered entirely worthy of cherishing, whether considered separately or together.

In the next two chapters aspects of both versions of history will be considered. But first it might be well to acknowledge that there is a danger in lingering too long in guilty contemplation of our particular story as seen from the point of view of the 'others'. For reconciliation does not necessarily or automatically come about simply as a result of our rehearsing the past or even in rearranging our lives in the light of what a guilty conscience is bringing to light. Judas Iscariot could not live with his guilty conscience; the Afrikaners are being driven mad by theirs.

J.M. Coetzee's novel, *Waiting for the Barbarians*, illustrates this point in the form of a contemporary parable.[4] The novel is about a weary, compromised, once-sensitive colonial governor who is jolted into sympathy with the empire's victims long after it is too late for any protest of his to be taken seriously. The native girl he has taken into his house brings to expression the whole gamut of fatal attraction, jealousy and contempt felt by the servant of empire for the subject people. His are 'the confused actions of an aging foreigner who picks her up off the streets and instals her in his apartment so that he can now kiss her feet, now browbeat her, now anoint her with exotic oils, now ignore her, now sleep in her arms all night, now moodily sleep apart'. The girl, who scarcely speaks at all in the novel is bemused by all this; in his treatment of her, he is sporadically and feebly attempting to expiate wrongs done by his empire to her native people. But his attempt at expiation is as unwholesome and in the end ineffective as the quixotic act of rebellion against the system which loses him his post and lands him in prison. He gains nothing from that gesture but humiliation and suffering. The people of the town gain nothing; they scarcely seem even to realise that he has done anything positive anyway. As the book ends, he is neither saved nor purified. There is no catharsis, even as he determines to take out to the desert again the poplar slips with hieroglyphics on them which he had years earlier dug up at a nearby archaeological site and has been attempting to construe and rearrange. They are the plundered records of a time in this land before the coming of the empire he represents, a civilisation which is as closed a book to the people of the town today as it is to him. Returning them to their place in the sand-covered site from which he took them is about all that he has conclusively determined to do by the end of the book—a sort of tribute to the people's pre-history, a history taken out of history.

His anointing of the girl, his obsessive study of the marks on the poplar slips, his ill thought-out and uncontrolled protest against the process of imperial justice he is supposed to serve—all of these are doomed to pathetic ineffectiveness. In a transitory moment of self-knowledge at the close of the book he thinks:

> I wanted to live outside history. I wanted to live outside the history that empire imposes on its subjects, even its lost subjects. I never wished it for the barbarians that they should have the history of empire laid upon them. How can I believe that that is a cause for shame?[5]

Of course it is not. But what is unavoidable for him is the burden of history that is laid on him, which cannot be sloughed off by any of the quirky or quixotic actions he has taken. Perhaps that is the 'something' which he confesses has been staring him in the face, 'and still I do not see it'. On our last glimpse of him he is watching children building a snowman. 'Like much else nowadays. I leave it feeling stupid, like a man who lost his way long ago, but passes on along a road that may lead nowhere.'[6]

In his case, it will almost certainly lead nowhere, because he no longer has the capacity to engage with the history he is inescapably part of otherwise than by uncontrolled and self-indulgent protests. In his case, protest serves only to arouse suspicions in his superiors as to his 'soundness'. His tragedy is that the mildly petulant objection to current imperial practice, which it gives him a kick to make and which leaves him feeling better for a little while, does not exculpate him. His years as magistrate, during which he enjoyed the beauty of the place and indulged a civilised taste for archaeology, were as fundamentally corrupt as his bachelor life was mildly so. But even the dim recognition of that fact does not lead him to a constructive reconstruction of his own life or a substantial critique of the system. It leads simply to what we have described.

Coetzee's novel serves to remind those who are serious about the resolution of conflict to acknowledge that memory in itself is not necessarily salvific. The New Testament writers are quite clear about this, as we see in the paradigmatic story of early disciples, portrayed in Matthew 14:22–34. Seeing a figure approaching them over the water, they shout out 'It is a ghost!' Simon Peter, however, says 'Lord, if it is you'—that is, you and not a ghost—'bid me come to you on the water.' In this passage, as elsewhere in the New Testament, the sea symbolises death and that dark abyss of meaninglessness through which Jesus has gone and which he is believed to have overcome. The risen Lord accordingly invites Simon Peter, the prototypical disciple, to come to him over the water, i.e. on the road which had led him to crucifixion and death. He invites the disciple into his risen present and future.

This passage poetically reflects on the actual experience of Simon Peter the disciple who, when all the rest ran away from the Garden of Gethsemane at the arrest of Jesus, alone of all of them 'followed at a distance . . . to see the end.' But in the courtyard of Caiaphas the high priest, his nerve failed. He denied his association with the prisoner, but when the cock crew, 'he went out and wept bitterly.'

The walking-on-the-water passage (Matthew 14:28–32), though apparently a part of the story of Jesus' life and Peter's pre-crucifixion experience, is really a reflexion on the significance of his experience of the risen Lord. This short passage suggests that the one who is locked into his memories, into remorseful and repeated reflection on his own disgraceful story, is set free from that insofar as he now entrusts himself to the present and future of the one who has overcome the sharpness of death, gone under the water of death and now walks upon it. His immediate circumstances, symbolised by the waves, strike terror into Peter and he starts to sink, but the strong arm of the risen one restores him to the boat with the rest of the community and to a future with them.

It is important to notice the conditional clause with which Simon Peter prefaces his request to his Lord to call him out on the sea: 'If it is you . . . ' i.e. 'If you are more than the ghost of a disturbing memory from an irredeemable past, then call me to you.' Peter wants to become part of his Lord's present and future, even though his own present and past overwhelm him. But, as long as he keeps his eye on the risen one, he does not sink.

This story of Matthew's serves as an exemplary paradigm for the Christian, in that it invites us to consider that our hag-ridden histories of treachery and betrayal can only be transcended when re-contextualised in terms of another story altogether. That other story is the history of the 'loser', Jesus of Nazareth, hailed by faith as vindicated and risen from the dead. Such re-contextualising radically alters our understanding of past and present and invites us to a process of 'subsequent insight'. In none of the gospels does the risen Christ appear to Caiaphas or Pilate or to those who plotted his death, in order to frighten them, settle old scores or turn the tables. In the resurrection narratives what *they* did is no longer central, but rather what *he* is going on to do and to be. On the other hand, the risen Christ does appear to his mostly quite unsatisfactory pupils and friends with a new agenda, or with the original one strangely uninterrupted by death. Their betrayals and failures do not set the agenda for his future. He has risen above all these things and now he 'goes before them into Galilee'. He invites disciples to join him there: it is an invitation to transcend the treadmill of 'winners' and 'losers' by reference to the history of this particular 'loser' and to the nature and character of his 'victory'.

But before returning to that theme or developing it in a later chapter, we should perhaps first look at the peculiar character of the nationalist and unionist ideologies themselves and at the version of history which sustains each of them. Then we may perhaps consider how they can be transcended in the context of this other story.

2

The Function of the Story: (1) Protestant-Unionist

The more common pattern of origin tales

In order to understand what is peculiar about the Ulster Protestant-unionist story, it has really to be compared with the origin tales celebrated most commonly by other peoples.

In telling the story of how they came into being in the first place or of how they came to be in 'possession' of the land they now occupy, most human societies trace their origin and consequently their right to the land, right back to the story of the first people in the world, to the gods and sometimes to creation itself. Ancient Israel is a case in point; and it is a case worth pondering for a moment. According to that story, the ancestor Jacob/Israel went down to Egypt and his offspring were later enslaved there, only to escape from their oppressor through the saving power of Yahweh their God. Their story forms the kernel of what came to be the dominant origin tale of ancient Israel, and this is the story celebrated in Israel's cult.[1] But it appears that this history was later extended backwards in time by the inclusion of originally unrelated sagas concerning the heroes of various tribes resident in the Palestinian homeland (Samson of Dan, Jephthah of Gilead, Gideon of the Abiezrites and others). These figures were set chronologically end to end to form a 'succession' of judges of Israel, even though in fact some of them must have been contemporaries. Anterior to the judges were placed the ancient sagas concerning Jacob, Isaac and that original ancestor Abraham who had left his home in Ur of the Chaldees to cross the fertile crescent westward. In due course, even this history was to be preceded by setting in sequence myths concerning the earliest days of the race which, in their original setting, would have had no chronological sequence whatever.[2]

This process had the effect of taking the history of the Hebrews right back to the first man and the first woman and to the creation of the world. Of course, this process of retrojection also served a cultural and political function; for a good deal of this history-writing took its present form from circa 1000 BCE during the reigns of David and his son

Solomon, when the Kingdom of Judah and Israel was expanding to include a number of neighbouring peoples. Israelites had to be reassured about the significance of Israel's place in the great scheme of things, and clearly it was desirable that their tributary peoples should also be impressed. Israel's own history was being set in the centre of what was then understood to be the history of the world.

The endeavour to push back the history of one's own dynasty or people to the earliest possible date has many parallels in other cultures. In early Christian Ireland, for instance, the learned class centered in the monasteries actually pressed earlier Christian historiography and the biblical history into service in order to take their own story back to the beginning of time. Rather like the author of *Judges*, these learned men wove together in a consecutive sequence stories which had been largely timeless and without chronology in the pre-Christian oral tradition. The origin tales of individual *tuatha*,[3] myths of the pagan gods, heroic sagas etc. all simply belonged to the old days and the beginning of time. No attempt appears originally to have been made to link them in chronological sequence. Irish scholars were first encouraged in this endeavour to place them in sequence by their reading of the Old Testament and, of course, by their acquaintance with the chronicle of Eusebius. Eusebius' chronicle had attempted to deal with the chronology of 'world' history by dating an event in one place by reference to events in another. Thus an event in some other part of the Mediterranean could be plotted in terms of its having occurred when so-and-so was tyrant of Athens or X and Y were tribunes in Rome. Irish scholars in effect rose to the challenge presented to them by the biblical history and Eusebius to slot Irish traditions into this overall scheme. Their historiographical endeavour was first given a name in modern times by Eoin Mac Néill; he called it 'synthetic history'.[4]

'Synthetic history' grew in inventiveness as time went on. But it is surely significant that what was probably its greatest flowering took place in the eleventh and twelfth centuries when attempts were being made to create a single kingdom out of a politically fragmented island. A homogeneous learned class which transcended the 'frontiers' between the multitudinous 'political' units in Ireland and Gaelic Scotland provided a cultural unity. This class, by their very existence, anticipated at the cultural level the political unity which Brian Bóroimhe and others tried and failed to establish. In a sense, they failed politically where the scholars of the reigns of David and Solomon succeeded. They did however succeed in setting Ireland's story into the widest and most significant context possible by retrojecting it to the time of Adam and Eve and the creation of the world.

Afrikaner and Ulster protestant history

But not all communities find it desirable to retroject their history to the beginning of time in quite this way. The Afrikaners, for instance, appear to show little interest in their origins in the Netherlands. The same applies to the descendants of the Huguenot refugees who came to South Africa post-1685, with reference to their point of origin in France. In marked and even proud contrast with the English South Africans, they do not look beyond the bounds of Africa in order to understand themselves. What happened to their forebears on the soil of Africa is their 'glory' and has determined their present. The realisation that whatever future they have must be lived in Africa gives an urgency and poignancy to their determination to hold on to what they have.

In much the same way Ulster Protestants have understood themselves primarily in terms of their *Irish* experience. Of very recent years it has become quite common for them to proclaim themselves to be 'British', or to build up the persona of the 'Ulster Scot'. But very few of those who bear Scottish surnames have any idea at all of where in Scotland they might have come from. Of course it is true that the proximity of Britain, the influx of Scottish workers into Belfast during the nineteenth century, and the continuous emigration to Britain has maintained a contact between Ulster and Britain for which there is no parallel as between the Afrikaners on the one hand and Holland or France on the other. Nevertheless, significant history in the view of the Ulster Protestant-unionist is not that of their forebears in England or Scotland. Significant history is the events, tragic and triumphant, which happened on Irish soil—the drowning of the Protestant women in 1641, the siege of Derry, the Covenant of 1912 and the gun-running at Larne. It is an extended saga of conquest and endurance. The agonising dilemma of the northern Protestant, like that of the Afrikaner, lies in the fact that as a community they have no other home to go to. Whatever it holds, the loyalists' future lies in Ireland, in a country they do not care to name for fear it should lay claim to them in some unacceptable way. It lies in the province of Ulster, which they do name, but claim exclusively, even though they know quite well that they are sharing it with a substantial number of others who see that province as simply one part of Ireland.

Another curious parallel between the Afrikaner and the Ulster Protestant manifests itself precisely at this point. They have both expressed their self-understanding in terms of another history altogether: a prototypical history in which, by common assent, God was uniquely active, i.e. the history of Israel, a people at once at home and not at home in the land they occupy. Like the Afrikaners and the Ulster Protestants, the Israelites were claiming a promised land which others stubbornly insisted on seeing as their home. This is in part what gives Israel's story so powerful an applicability to the situations both of the Afrikaners and of the Ulster Protestants of planter stock.

The centrepiece of Afrikaner historical self-consciousness, never forgotten for long in the school classroom, is the Great Trek of 1837. In that year the Voortrekker leader, Piet Retief, posted a manifesto in which he set forth the reasons why he and those with him were leaving the south and pressing inland and away from the alien jurisdiction of the British. Of course the English of the Cape saw the Afrikaners as a bunch of reactionary and backward red-necks. But the 'red-necks' saw themselves quite differently, i.e. as the children of Israel fleeing from Pharaoh's bondage in Egypt, their faces set for the wilderness to serve God there. In 1880, at the very start of the Transvaal War, an Afrikaner minister could still preach this equation:

> Behold the armies of the salvation of the Lord. We are as Israel of old—before us lay the Red Sea, behind us was the Egyptian host and on either side of us were lofty mountains. We could but look up and cry to God, and he heard our voice.[5]

An opportunity to 'spoil the Egyptians' came later, during the South African War when, as has been claimed, the Boers invented modern guerrilla war tactics and inflicted humiliating losses on the forces of the British Empire. As time went on, however, the weight of their superior resources won the war for the British. But the concentration camps in which so many Afrikaner women and children starved to death were a grim price to pay for victory. The memory of those camps still fuels Afrikaner resentment to this day, much as the atrocities of the Black and Tans do in this country. The story of persecution and endurance leads finally to the story of Boer victory at the election of 1948 which returned the National Party to power.

By the nature of the case, written sources do not tell us as much as we would wish to know of how the Great Trek appeared to the real losers—the Zulu, the Xhosa or the Basutho peoples. But in the great equation of Afrikaner political theology, the blacks are only the children of Ham, cursed by his father Noah (Genesis 9:20–27) and condemned to perpetual servitude or at best, by a divine providence, destined to develop separately under the patronage of the sons of Shem and Japhet. Moreover, according to Afrikaner historiography, there were in any case very few, if any, black people in southern Africa at the end of the seventeenth century. So, the argument runs, who is to say whose land it really is—especially when you take into consideration that the 'Bantu' is racially incapable of cultivating it as God has ordained it should be? Interestingly, exactly the same claim has been made recently with reference to Ulster in the years immediately preceding the plantation.[6] Daniel F. Malan, the first National Party prime minister of South Africa in 1948, who was of course an eloquent exponent of apartheid, spoke of his people's history and destiny in the following terms:

> The last 100 years have witnessed a miracle, behind which must lie a divine plan. Indeed, the history of the Afrikaner reveals a will and a determination which makes one feel that Afrikanerdom is not the work of men but of God.[7]

There is in itself nothing unusual about the quest for parallels between one's own history and that of the Hebrew people. It is found all over Europe in the medieval period, not least in Ireland in the wake of the Anglo-Norman invasion, in the work of the *filí* and the annalists. In the seventeenth-century Jacobites engaged in this activity as readily as their opponents. Poetry in English, Irish and Scottish Gaelic nourishes hopes for the restoration of James VII and II by reference to King David's flight from Jerusalem (=James' flight from London) and his eventual return after the death of his usurping son, Absalom (=William and Mary).

Wherever Protestantism took root, the Old Testament and the history of Israel usually came in for renewed attention and study. This may well be because Calvinists, in particular, believed that God's dealings with ancient Israel under the 'old covenant' in some way foreshadowed God's dealings with the Church under the new. Protestants in general, but in particular the English Puritans and the Scottish Covenanters, understood themselves precisely as a new Israel.

The banners of Orange Lodges and the Black Institution displayed proudly on parade on the Twelfth of July and other occasions through the year, do not all have biblical themes, but many do. Indeed, they are instructive if we are to see our way into the loyalist mind sympathetically and clearly.

The first thing we notice is that the themes depicted are highly selective and, at first sight, even arbitrary. In fact, however, there is a curious thread of unity discernible in the series.[8] Nor is this surprising once we know that at initiation into a Royal Arch Purple Chapter or one of the degrees of the Black Institution, the initiate is called upon to play the role of one or more of the characters in a drama in which biblical stories are played out. Two persons known as 'lecturers', who act as masters of ceremonies in all this, commonly read out the particular stories and give a 'sound' interpretation and application of them. The stories chosen which in turn find visual representation in the banners, are designed to offer instructive and encouraging parallels between the position and plight of the people of Israel or representative Hebrew individuals on the one hand, and the position and plight of the Protestant people of Ireland, today and yesterday on the other. But their primary importance lies in the fact that they provide a divine sanction for Protestant dominance.

Certain themes may be selected, as being of particular significance:

(1) Individuals or the people of Israel as a whole are in a strange land, or in their own land which has apostasised. Their faithfulness is rewarded: one thinks here of Daniel, who steadfastly opened his window toward Jerusalem at the hour of prayer in spite of the orders of the king to the contrary. As a result he is thrown into the lions' den. Next morning he is found unharmed, and his accusers and their families are punished. Also popular is Joseph: sold into slavery in Egypt by his brothers, in the end he saves his brothers from starvation. Banners representing events in the life of Moses are particularly important: but centrally important of course are the escape from Egypt, the parting of the Red Sea and the giving of the Ten Commandments, seen as a prototype of the Bible itself upon which Protestants exclusively depend. One may recall what Aaron the father of the priesthood was up to while his brother was on the mountain! The journey through the desert is open to allegorical treatment in terms of the Protestant people's sufferings and backslidings. Another favourite banner portrays Jacob's dream as he sleeps at Luz on the stone pillow and sees a ladder set up from earth to heaven with angels ascending and descending on it. On waking he sets the stone on end, calls the place Bethel and says: 'Surely, the Lord is in this place and I knew it not.' Jacob has gained the favour of God and, by tricking his brother Esau, the blessing of his father Isaac: now he is in a strange country on the run and receives promises that his offspring will inherit the land. Jacob is also, incidentally,

off to marry 'one of his own', not like Esau who had married Hittite women who 'made life bitter' for Isaac and Rebecca.

Elijah, who so often appears being fed by the ravens at the brook Cherith, is the type of those who remain faithful when the very king himself, under the influence of his wife Jezebel and her *foreign* religion, has apostasised. When Elijah imagines he is the only one who has not bowed the knee to Baal, he is assured that there are in fact 7,000 who have not. In a contest with the *priests* of Baal, this prophet calls down fire from heaven and has the satisfaction of personally dispatching 850 of the idolatrous priests.

(2) This brings us to the related theme of the cleansing of the people from idolatry by those who have never been seduced by fancy ideas from outside. Note the popularity in this regard of Jehu, whose killing of his rival Jehoram is symbolised by the emblem of an arrow piercing through a heart on many an orange chart and collarette. Jehu is the counter-king anointed by Elijah after Ahab's death to clean the kingdom up and prefigures William III.

(3) The smallness of the faithful remnant: this is a common theme throughout the narrative and the prophetic literature of the Old Testament. It receives reassuring iconographic treatment in banners which portray David the shepherd boy selecting the five smooth stones at the brook for his sling or show him decapitating the Philistine giant Goliath. Sometimes this banner has over it the chilling quotation (from whom?), 'He who would be free must strike the blow.'

Almost equally chilling is the representation of Gideon who, in the campaign against the Midianites and Amalekites who have over-run the land, is told by God more than once to reduce them till he has finally only 300 left. The banner shows these men, each carrying a sword and a pitcher inside which is a barely concealed lamp. At the sound of Gideon's trumpet, each man is to blow his own trumpet, break his pitcher, thus revealing his lamp, and shout aloud: 'The sword of the Lord and of Gideon!' What application that can be given in a situation such as ours can only be guessed at.

(4) According to the theology which informs their banners, it is just possible for outsiders to come into the fold, even though they are gentiles. The two outstanding examples are women, however. One is the quite exemplary Ruth who has married in and who insists on returning to Israel from her native Moab with her mother-in-law Naomi after they have both been widowed. She

adopts the God of Israel as her God, and all goes well with her. She is a forebear of David and therefore also of Jesus. These stories offer some hope for a compliant Catholic bride. The other woman is Rahab the harlot of Jericho who is good to the Israelite spies—to the extent that she betrays her own city, and is therefore spared when everyone else in the city is slaughtered. One assumes there is a lesson for Catholic women here too!

Suffice to say, that Orange and Black iconography in emblems, banners and rituals does not exhaust the possibilities. For the Old Testament in particular is a rich mine for allegory and direct parallel. Sermons still exploit these possibilities imaginatively even today, and Orange songs give sometimes fairly crude expression to it too as, for instance, the song *Dolly's Brae* in which Roman Catholic priests are presented as distributing 'the wafer god among the Philistines'.

We have already noted the paramount importance, in terms of their understanding of their own history, of events which took place on the soil of Ireland. In spite of the significance of events like 1641 or (to a much smaller extent) 1798 or 1916 or even 'southern neutrality' in 1939–45 or the 'so-called' civil rights campaign, all of which go to show the fundamental deviousness and treachery in the hearts of the Catholic people, the overwhelmingly significant event in loyalist history is the siege of Derry. It has everything: a beleaguered community, an indecisive traitor in the midst i.e. Governor Lundy, who is paralleled throughout loyalist history by subsequent weak, gullible or self-seeking leaders; suffering and endurance on the part of the citizens; good young lads (the Apprentices) whose hearts are in the right place and who, by going against orders and slamming the gates shut, do what the leadership could not bring itself to do; and, finally, the rescue of the 'Maiden City' through the instrumentality of William's ship the *Mountjoy* breaking the boom. This action with its quasi-sexual overtones, no doubt acts as a kind of archetype for the rough talk and action of perhaps Edward Carson and certainly Ian Paisley, as has been suggested by Dr Antony Buckley.[9]

Outside the walls (but also, rather alarmingly, increasingly inside the walls) the 'others' worshipped images and said prayers at holy wells—in every way bringing to mind the idolaters in the land of Israel, serving their idols and 'bowing down under every green tree'. And, outside in the darkness, they could be heard singing—actually enjoying themselves, apparently untroubled by their invincible ignorance, unbowed under their troubles and, as the decades passed, begetting ever more children against that day when majorities might have to be heard.

Of course, it would be quite unrealistic and inaccurate to suggest that the more recherché of these biblical, or for that matter, seventeenth-century parallels are part of the consciousness of every loyalist. Not every worshipper at an Orange service is daily searching the scriptures for parallels, precedents and portents. Nevertheless a basic story does exist within the covers of the Old Testament, susceptible of elaboration, and available to give resonance to the prosaic realities of everyday life.

We have already noted parallels between the self-understandings of Afrikaners and Ulster Protestants. It is not surprising to find a confessional background in common between the two; for Calvinism has been the dominant form of Christian presence in South Africa among the Afrikaners and in Ulster among the Protestants.

It has left marks upon both for good and ill. The Dutch Reformed Church in South Africa began to cut its links with the mother Church in Holland just at the time when the latter Church's theology was beginning to feel some impact from the Enlightenment.[10] Indeed, by 1817 the theology of Dort was no longer binding upon all ministers and office-bearers.[11] The establishment of an independent seminary at Stellenbosch in 1859 was largely in the interests of moderating the influence of liberal theology from Europe. But there was at the same time another influence from the outside, affecting primarily though not exclusively the English-speaking population. It was the new evangelical enthusiasm of the Scottish ministers who arrived in the 1820s. Their emphasis on personal decision and conversion fitted ill with scholastic Calvinism which laid emphasis primarily on God's predestining decision and left little to personal decision. And yet, in South Africa as in other parts of the world the two managed to coexist.

Certainly they came to coexist within Irish Presbyterianism. In Ireland insistence on subscription to the *Westminster Confession of Faith* of 1649 served first to isolate and then to drive out those who found themselves unable to subscribe to it as the uniquely authentic interpretation of the faith. By the middle of the nineteenth century, Ulster Protestantism was shorn of its theological liberals and most of its political ones.[12] Carefully monitored subscription to the *Confession* by elders as well as ministers served for a time to insulate Irish Presbyterianism against theological liberalism and biblical criticism. Of course, as the nineteenth century gave way to the twentieth, neither theological liberalism nor the findings of biblical scholarship could be ignored. In 1929 Ernest Davey, a professor in the Presbyterian Church's seminary in Assembly's College, Belfast was tried for heresy. Davey was acquitted; but the Presbyterian

Church is arguably still recovering from the shock, and the trial has tended to encourage self-censorship in ministers and has handed over the theological initiative to the conservative and the cautious.[13]

But another factor, already referred to with reference to the Scottish immigrant ministers in South Africa, also manifested itself in Irish Protestantism in the middle of the nineteenth century, i.e. evangelical revivalism, which came to a sometimes quite spectacular flowering in the revival of 1859. And again in Ireland, as elsewhere, there was an inevitable tension between those who had been brought up on the predestinating theology of the *Shorter Catechism* and the *Westminster Confession* and those who now preached for conversion and were rewarded by numerous converts.

How were these two groups to settle down together? Could there be a *modus vivendi*? Certainly, in their attitudes to ethical and political questions there was no real cleavage between them. In their view of scripture, the two groups were often equally biblicist. But their theologies were in fact poles apart. A man like William Gibson, minister of Rosemary Street Church in Belfast and then a professor in Assembly's College, wrote a book about the 1859 revival which he entitled *The Year of Grace*.[14] Isaac Nelson, minister of Donegall Street Church produced a counterblast, *The Year of Delusion*, in which he expressed his alarm, theological and temperamental, in the face of the emotionalism of the revival and its heavy emphasis on the human response.[15] The controversy about 'assurance of faith' which followed the revival, really centered again on the status of enthusiasm and spiritual experience as criteria. Henry Cooke, the great champion of orthodoxy and of political unionism in the Synod of Ulster appears to have found no grounds of contradiction here, but others did.[16]

It may well be appropriate at this point to explain that the *Westminster Confession* of 1649, accepted by Irish Presbyterians as a uniquely authoritative statement of Christian doctrine, holds to the doctrine of predestination. This doctrine has its roots in the writing of the apostle Paul and of Augustine. In those writers it is enunciated in order to state clearly that God has called men and women in Christ from all eternity, though it is conceded that not all will in the end be included in the number of the elect. The theologians who drew up the *Westminster Confession* drew the conclusion that not only had the omniscient God, by what they referred to as the 'eternal decrees', foreordained some to eternal life, God has also from all eternity predestined others to damnation. No action on the part of human beings, good or evil, could alter these decrees. This doctrine was known as '*double* predestination'.

This is the teaching of the *Shorter Catechism*, prepared by the authors of the *Westminster Confession*, and learned by rote right down to our own day. However, even in spite of the Catechism's prestigious position, it is true to say that in the course of the nineteenth century, if not earlier, large numbers both of theological 'liberals' and 'conservatives' began to be uneasy about the doctrine of double predestination—liberals because it offended the 'enlightened conscience' and conservatives because its inflexibility ran the risk of cutting across the whole appeal of evangelical preaching for decisions for or against Christ.

Actually, evangelicals continued to preach for decisions, more or less without regard for the 'eternal decrees' of God. Nevertheless, within evangelical circles the doctrine of election continued to serve at least two purposes—one practical and theological, and the other social and political.

Practically and theologically, it served to rationalise the stubborn fact that there do appear to be unregenerate people. Even in the most godly families, it was observed that there are those who in spite of every opportunity fall from grace, while others reared in the same household 'confirm their election' by exemplary conduct. The conviction that some are from all eternity predestined to be saved and others to be damned, at least made sense of such a case.

More significant, however, from the point of view of our study is the use to which the doctrine came increasingly to be put socially and politically. At this level, it provided a theological rationale for the use, already referred to, of the Old Testament history of the chosen people, particularly with reference to their treatment of the people of the land, most of whom could be considered as lost in a state of invincible ignorance. As we shall see later, their ignorance and unregenerate nature actually justified the elect/Protestant people in having taken their land in the first place, but also set a great question mark against the practicability and advisability of seeking to convert them. One may say in conclusion that the resolution to the conflict lay in the privatising of the preaching for conversion and the politicizing of the doctrine of predestination.

Before leaving this subject it is worth considering briefly how the Orange Order functioned as the institutional embodiment of this politicisation of double predestination. It should be noted (a) that it has been an umbrella organisation, a pseudo-Church which brought together those who variously attended church and meeting. At its own meetings 'in lodge' it provided ritual of a character missing both in the Presbyterian congregation and in the self-consciously Low Church liturgy of the Church of Ireland; (b) it was/is of fixed membership, *open only to*

Protestants who have never been Roman Catholics. Being so fixed in membership it takes into its own life something of the election theology which for reasons we have been discussing was receiving less emphasis in the evangelical preaching of the Churches themselves; (c) being dedicated to the defence of Protestantism and the Protestant succession to the throne, it has had no qualms—in fact, it had no alternative—but to draw the political and *communal* implications of what its members understood to be close to the heart of the matter, i.e. Protestant ascendancy.

But privatising and pietism continued to be features of Protestant religion within the Churches and the sects of Ireland, whether of the so-called 'liberal' or 'conservative' variety. Indeed, so long as their religion could be regarded as essentially a personal matter, a question of personal experience, 'liberals' and 'conservatives' found it possible to coexist. There was often a class differentiation involved between the two, though not always. Liberals being for the most part more affluent, have increasingly provided the leadership in this century both of the Presbyterian Church and the Church of Ireland. But the leadership needed the mass of more conservative clergy and people for credibility.

Dr Antony Buckley describes what he watched on the 11th July in what he calls 'Long Stone' in the predominantly Protestant area of Listymore in north Antrim.[17] There are two villages in Listymore: Long Stone and Killycarnon. The people of Long Stone regard those of Killycarnon as 'snooty' and 'stuck-up' whereas the people of Killycarnon view the Long Stoners as on the 'rough side'. Dr Buckley describes how, at midnight on the '11th Night' in question, about two dozen men took two Lambeg Drums out of the Long Stone Orange hall and set off for Killycarnon, beating the drums and followed by a cheerful crowd of one hundred or so, 'predominantly but not exclusively teenagers'. Dr Buckley comments:

> The Lambeg drum in this case was indeed affirming a distinctively Protestant identity; but it was also doing something else. It was asserting the values, much prized among many in Long Stone, of 'plainness', masculinity, straightforwardness, bluntness and good fellowship, believed by some to be not much in evidence in the 'snooty' village of Killycarnon.[18]

In his anxiety to make the perfectly good point that more was involved than asserting Protestant identity or even dominance, Dr Buckley claims that what was coming to the surface during that couple of hours was 'the dislike of the comparatively poor for the comparatively rich, of the teenaged young for the figures who represent authority and, more specifically, of inebriated young males for more upright citizens'. No doubt these things are *present*: but what gives them impetus? The *resentment* of the comparatively poor, the teenaged, the inebriated young males is directed at the comparatively comfortable, conceivably rather complacent people on 'their own side' who live the way they do in Killycarnon because there are other people living in the less affluent conditions of Long Stone. When the chips are down Killycarnon needs Long Stone and, keeping them awake at 2 o'clock in the morning to the beat of a Lambeg drum is a good way of reminding them of the fact. That is also Paisley's message to the Malone Road and affluent unionism. That is why, when morning comes, they hate him so much. They know it is true.

In the end of the day, it has been more important than anything else to belong to the elect people and state that clearly. Up to the present it has been the peculiar strength of Ian Paisley that he has headed the Free Presbyterian Church as well as leading the Democratic Unionist Party and increasingly become the 'voice of unionism'. Clearly his political following includes a majority of people who do not belong to the Free Presbyterian Church. Many of them may never even have heard him preach—never mind making a decision for Christ at one of his services. But they will be politically sound through membership of the Orange Order or one of the unionist parties. That is, in a different sense, a public matter and one of paramount importance. It may even serve to deflect attention from denominational affiliation or religious convictions which are not so 'sound', but which 'matter' less because they belong to the area of individual conviction and personal experience.

Attitudes toward the ecumenical movement, however, are not deemed to belong to the private sphere. For these involve 'truck with Rome' and with the political 'enemies of Ulster'. It is worth remembering that the ecumenical movement is suspect among many Ulster Protestants—not because it involves being civil to Roman Catholics or even because it aims to respect their conscientious personal convictions, but because it appears to concede what are called the political claims of that Church and by extension of its adherents. To allow their story a hearing alongside the Protestant-unionist one might well be to appear to concede the political claims inherent in their version of history.

To that version of history we now turn.

3

The Function of the Story: (2) Catholic-Nationalist; (3) The 'Protestant Nation'; (4) The 1916 Proclamation

(1) The Catholic-nationalist

In the previous chapter we concentrated on the unionist story, its realisation, and the function which that realisation fulfils. In this chapter it is proposed briefly to consider the Catholic-nationalist tradition, the Anglo-Irish experience and the 1916 Proclamation and observe the function that their various stories have been made to serve. Problems do not arise simply because one group has one set of cherished memories and another group another. Nor are they solved simply by taking account of the fact that 'the anthology of the other is a book I hadn't reckoned with' as Iain Crichton Smith has confessed.[1] Of course in a community as rent asunder as ours has been, greater acquaintance with the others' story could scarcely fail to help and heal.[2] It would be especially useful if we were to make audible the experience—not alone of Catholics and Protestants, but also those of women, sexual minorities and the poor. But, as has already been suggested in chapter 1, the heartache and the hurt have their point of origin, not in the story itself, but in the *use* to which we put it. For every group's story has a *function*, it is there to serve, both internally in maintaining the fabric and morale of the group and its institutions, and externally in shaping the relationship of that group with others outside.

Internally, as far as Catholic nationalist Ireland is concerned, identity has rested on what students of comparative literature recognise as an *origin tale*, i.e. a story which justifies the present occupancy of land etc. in terms of a tale which explains how the ancestors came to be there in the first place.[3] The Gaelic tradition has relied on this foundation right from the beginning, as we have already seen in the previous chapter. The case for the primacy of the Gael was easier to make in Ireland than in Scotland, where various linguistic and cultural groups competed from the beginning of the historical period for primacy. Indeed the inauguration of Cinaed mac Ailpin as 'King of Picts and Scots' in 843AD[4] may be seen as the first attempt in a long series to create national unity out of cultural diversity. But in Ireland in the historical period, the Gaels and their language had for centuries no serious rival; their story was the story of Ireland.

More important, from our point of view, than the evidence of Old and Middle Irish literature however are the attitudes which survived through the last 400 years of conquest, subjection, acquiescence and re-assertion. The story, by means of which these attitudes are conveyed, is one made up almost exclusively of defeats and even betrayals—at Kinsale, at the Boyne and Aughrim and in Antrim town in 1798. Even 1916 is a defeat, from the jaws of which victory of a kind was snatched. But even that victory was incomplete: and the border is there to remind us all of that particular unresolved conflict. In all this the Catholic nationalist tradition is in marked contrast with the Orange one, which celebrates annually the *victory* at the Boyne in 1690 and the happy triumph of the raising of the siege of Derry.

When the Proclamation of 1916 speaks of the fact that 'in every generation the Irish people have asserted their right to national freedom and sovereignty' and goes on to say that 'six times during the past 300 years they have asserted it in arms', the drafters are in point of fact referring to risings which either fizzled out or were cruelly put down. In the last of those centuries (the nineteenth) it was increasingly Catholicism, rather than nationalism, which became for a majority the badge of Irishness. During that century the Irish language, which in the previous two and a half centuries had been deposed from one domain after another of public life, ceased even to be that of the majority of the common people when engaged in even the commonest pursuits. Catholicism, alone of all the causes and institutions to which most Irish people owed allegiance, was not defeated. Not surprisingly, given the course of Irish history, Catholicism provided a nationalist identity among the majority of those most energetically involved in the struggle for Home Rule or an independent State in the nineteenth century.

Eoin Mac Néill had drunk in the prevailing notions of language and nationality/language and culture which emanated from Herder and his disciples. Yet it has just been said of him that 'a strong sense of Catholicism informed [his] philosophy of Irish-Ireland throughout'. So writes Donal McCartney who then quotes MacNéill as follows:

> No course of events injurious to religion can possibly be helpful to the cause of spiritual nationality of which the League is the champion.[5]

A failure to hold the quest for an Irish state together with a cultural vision and vice versa arguably led to a situation, particularly in the growing Catholic middle class, where non-essential characteristics of 'Irishness' were seized upon as though they were of the essence. And the curious thing is that this happened both among those who were quite content with the attenuated cultural nationalism of Moore's Melodies and among those who were politically active in the struggle for Home Rule or even independence. Catholicism was the most common as well as the most substantial of these characteristics, of course.

The gradual identification of Catholicism with the demand for self-determination led people as different from one another as J. Biggar the Belfast butcher and Irish Party MP, and Roger Casement from Ballymena Castle, one sooner and the other later, to convert to Catholicism. In our own day, 'nationally minded' Protestants will testify to the well-intentioned efforts made by Catholic fellow-citizens to make them feel at home in the camp by reciting the names of Protestants of the past who, though this is not said, in *spite* of being Protestants, were on the 'right side'. Small wonder that the women and men of the north-east in the 1790s who wished to transcend the confessional question, are rarely mentioned, even by those who pride themselves on their 'republicanism'.[6]

Catholicism, the emphasis amounting sometimes almost to obsession on Gaelic blood and surnames, and the assumption which has lasted right down to our own time that a rural background is somehow more genuinely Irish than an urban one—these things are explicable historically, but they are reprehensible. For side by side with more benign explanations, must lie the suspicion that this line of thought about land and race owes a good deal less to the Gaelic preoccupation with *sloinneadh* (genealogy) than it does to the romanticism of eighteenth- and nineteenth-century central Europe. It must surely go without saying that *sloinneadh* (the naming of one's ancestors) operated in the patriarchal society of say, Fermanagh or Tipperary in the seventeenth century, in a way quite different from the way it does in the Dublin suburbs in the late nineteenth. The Irish middle class by the end of the nineteenth century had lost fluency in the language, and was no longer living on the land. It required some other tangible link to the land it felt to be its own to be forged and this was, I believe, done by a romanticism which elsewhere, but here too, led to slogans of *Blut und Boden, Faith and Fatherland.*

Some of those engaged in revolutionary politics in the 1790s—particularly in and around Belfast, like Thomas Russell—recognised in the language an antidote to what was happening. A century later, the wide-ranging membership of the Gaelic League from its foundation until 1915 is further evidence of the same recognition. Efforts were being made in the North even as late as 1988 to rescue the Irish language for all the people in the face of those who assume it is especially the property of one political point of view—notably in some of the submissions to the Belfast City Plan.[7] But can they succeed?

Too often the question as to who is 'really Irish' (itself a question born of insecurity) boils down to preoccupation with inessentials, and concentration on such shaky criteria as the surname of a person. Such concentration has nothing to do with Gaelic ways of thought, as can readily be seen by a comparison of the Irish and the Scottish Gaels in this respect. Of course, it was (and with older people still is) the custom in the Irish as in the Scottish Gaeltacht, to identify oneself in terms of *sloinneadh* (genealogy) going back seven generations as, for instance, Tomás Ó Criomhthain does in *An tOileánach*. But any impartial observer would agree that *sloinneadh* is more important in Scotland than in Ireland. One suspects that this is due to historical factors, the most important of which is the continuity of the clan system up to 1746 in the highlands and the continuity of land holding by the old chiefly families even thereafter, as opposed to the radical change that took place in land-holding in the course of the seventeenth century in Ireland. In Scotland a family might come to be in reduced circumstances, but that very fact made it all the more important that they should be able to show how near they were in blood relationship to the chief. In Ireland, where the application of a confessional litmus paper, either brought about the exile of the chiefly family or relegated them to a place alongside others of lower rank, *sloinneadh* lost its *practical* application and, where it survived, was no more than the expression of dull resentment or, later, sentimentality. In other words, it functioned in the Gaeltacht of Scotland in a way that it did not in Ireland.

I have tried to show elsewhere[8] the way in which the *filí* (poets and historians) of Ireland and the *bards* of Scotland differ in their deployment of the rhetoric of vituperation. In summary, it may be observed that the Irish employ new terms of abuse from the seventeenth century onwards—unknown in Gaelic Scotland—*Clann Liútair, Clann Chailbhin, eiricigh* (heretics) to refer to those of a new language and confessional allegiance who now held tracts of land in Ireland. Such terminology is unknown in the works of the Scottish Gaelic bards, though clearly they were living in a country and in a century no less drastically affected by the confessional hostilities of the time. The fact is that in Scotland nobody lost land on the application of a confessional test: in Ireland they did, and for the most part permanently. Those who forfeited their estates in Scotland did so on political grounds, and they nearly always got them back. This crucial difference between Ireland and Gaelic Scotland may serve to show the importance of a functional approach to the study of the role of story. The story of confessional allegiance and the story of lost land became almost inextricably linked in Ireland in a way that they did not in Gaelic Scotland.

Popular Catholic nationalism has never had much time for those who are not Catholic unless pushed to it by the need to find friends or in the face of accusations of sectarianism. The realisation or re-enactment of this particular story has tended to be exclusive not inclusive.

(2) 'The Protestant nation'.

The Catholic people of Ireland could take for granted that the land was theirs and that they themselves belonged to it; the *task* of the surviving Catholic families of substance post-1691 was to establish their fitness to be part of the political nation. What has been called 'the Protestant nation' was in a different but complementary position. With so slender a demographic base and so short a history they came in time to feel the impulse to establish more certainly their relationship with the land they now controlled.

Military and economic self-confidence in the generations immediately after the traumatic events of 1689–91 allowed the Anglo-Irish the leisure to identify more closely with the country. As Liam de Paor puts it:

> The post-Revolution ascendancy, freed from the Jacobite threat to their property and privilege, enjoyed a brief period in which they conceived of themselves as the nation. In the first half of the century their hostility was directed chiefly at the aristocracy and gentry they had replaced. They paid much less heed to the lower orders of Catholics.[9]

Among the Anglo-Irish the view was canvassed that, contrary to what Catholic scholarly gentlemen like Charles O'Conor of Belanagare, Co. Roscommon were claiming for that Irish Golden Age which had preceded all invasions, the Irish were nothing more than incomers from Britain anyway.[10] The idea that they were inferior and were in any case now dying out was widely entertained during this period, but the demographic facts of life shattered that idea in the second half of the century.

Throughout the eighteenth century this new gentry took pride in the achievements of 'the Protestant nation'. They saw no reason to listen to Catholic antiquarians who claimed, on the evidence of history, that the dispossessed represented a stock which had every claim to be admitted to the rights and responsibilities of the political nation. As the century wore on, and particularly after the publication of James Macpherson's *Fragments* in 1760,[11] many among them began to appropriate the distant past. For this period they preferred to use the term 'Hibernian', rather than 'Irish'. The Protestant (i.e. Episcopalian) parliament in College Green was increasingly filled in its last decades with men who recognised that their interests, like those of the American colonists, did not always coincide with those of London. Furthermore, they smarted under the patronising behaviour of the London parliament and government. They were Irish; but they were Irish in a way that clearly distinguished them from the peasantry and from such of the Catholic gentlemanly families as had managed to survive the penal times.

The importance of Macpherson in the development of romantic cultural nationalism can scarcely be over-estimated.[12] Only one of the gentlemen who paid Macpherson to visit the highlands in search of the lost Gaelic epic was a Gaelic speaker.[13] The rest were representatives of the lowland oligarchy of churchmen and law-men who controlled the most important Scottish institutions post-1707, with little reference to London. These men were in search of what educated people considered the *sine qua non* of the 'civilised nation'—an epic.

The gentlemen of the Irish ascendancy who defended the authenticity of 'Ossian' were also engaging in more than a mere literary debate. They were laying claim to the immemorially old history of Ireland through an epic which (it was alleged) had been composed in the third century AD. In their view, the real inheritors of the heroic age that Ossian sang of were clearly not the highlanders or the Irish peasants of the eighteenth or early nineteenth centuries. The heirs of that age were the *literati* of Edinburgh or, in Ireland, the first members of the Royal Irish Academy and the Fellows of Trinity College. The defense of Macpherson and the appropriation of Ossian's epic is a clear indication that, in the end of the day, it is intolerable to those who develop pretensions to noble blood and aristocracy not to be able to show that they belong to the land as much as the land belongs to them.

In her remarkable and still unfortunately unpublished thesis, Linda Spencer[14] has shown how the lowland Scots and the north American settlers, once they had rendered the highlanders and native Americans militarily harmless, came to think of them as being the true Scots, the true Americans. The highlander and the native American, who are often portrayed as looking alike in contemporary drawings, lived beyond an identifiable frontier. As time passed, the frontier moved. After they had been subdued, romantics could see in them *natural* gentlemen. So Hugh Blair, professor in Edinburgh University and minister of the High Kirk, could write: 'Barbarity is a very equivocal term; it admits of many different forms and degrees, and though in all of them it excludes polished manners, it is however, not inconsistent with generous sentiments and tender affections.'[15]

Once the Gaels of Scotland had been defeated by the forces of 'civilisation', the highlanders could become 'noble'. George IV could don the kilt on his visit to Scotland in 1822. Walter Scott could glorify the highland chiefs quite uncritically. The way was open for Prince Albert and the Highland Gathering at Braemar and for his wife to speak of 'my dear highlanders'. But in Ireland the frontier was everywhere; the natives were over every hedge and even in the servants' hall.[16] That made the process of appropriating Ireland's past on the part of the 'Protestant nation' more difficult, but it did not altogether prevent it. Enough could be appropriated for the incomers' descendants to feel that they belonged every bit as much as those they had displaced.

The so-called 'Celtic Church' also came to serve a purpose in this process of acclimatisation. A selective study of the writings of the early Irish Church, the sacred sites of which had almost all been appropriated by the Church of Ireland, enabled Low Church Episcopalians to convince themselves that they were the spiritual heirs of Patrick, Brigid and Columcille,[17] and that the Celtic saints were Protestants before their time. Clearly the cluttered churches and superstitious practices of contemporary Catholicism were a corruption of the primitive purity of the early Church and the Celtic saints—a purity which had now been recovered in the Church of Ireland as by law established.

Though it could be argued that this process had some agreeable and, indeed, valuable results in the works of poets, antiquarians and even politicians and eventually led to the establishment of the Gaelic League in 1893,[18] on the whole the process of acclimatisation and appropriation on the part of the Anglo-Irish consistently dismissed the claims and mis-prized the identity of the Catholic majority. John Fitzgibbon, the Lord Chancellor, perceived accurately the dilemma of Grattan and the established Church 'patriots' of the Dublin parliament in the last two decades of the eighteenth century when he spoke of 'their inability to reconcile the continuation of their own perceived position as leaders of the nation with the aspirations and the inescapable fact of the existence of close on four million Catholics'.[19]

The story which the Anglo-Irish were now telling and realising in the process of satisfying themselves that they belonged to the land as much as it belonged to them, could not easily be made to tally with the resentful memories of those whose land they had taken.

(3) The 1916 Proclamation

The history alluded to, rather than re-told, in the Easter Proclamation of 1916 is there to justify the events of Easter Monday and the days following at the GPO. It aims to show that the rising was in a long line of justifiable attempts to establish an Irish State. The very term Saorstát Éireann implicitly and, in the writings of Eoin Mac Néill explicitly, assert that, even though Ireland had never been a modern nation State, in the remote past it had had its polity, its high kings, and its legal system which gave expression to its distinctive nationality.[20] When Pearse and Connolly made the decision to avoid further bloodshed in the rising by surrendering, Pearse handed over his sword to the British commanding officer. By that action Pearse was indicating and the commanding officer was in fact conceding that this was a *war*, not a rebellion. The claim to be a political nation was in that action being made, and conceded.

In whichever of the examples we have briefly taken (the Protestants of the North-East, the Anglo-Irish, the Gaels, those who fought in 1916 etc.), we have had to do with a group who are explaining and even seeking to justify their present in terms of the past. In a sense, the history of each is a *just so* story; it explains why things are the way they are and not some other way, why people are taking one course of action rather than another.

Sometimes the same events or persons are appropriated in Ireland by mutually opposed groups. So, in the case of Wolfe Tone,[21] we have a man who is annually commemorated on successive Sunday afternoons at Bodenstown, his burial-place, by Fianna Fáil, the Worker's Party, Sinn Féin and others. Each group justifies its contemporary stance in terms of what they understand to be his significance in the total history. It goes without saying that mutually opposed groups who have recourse to the same story will be particularly virulent in their mutual excommunications. Christians who look dispassionately over the last 400 years of Church history should acknowledge how easily this can happen.

Not surprisingly, commemoration varies greatly, both in style and content as between one society and another. Those who are used to one mode of commemoration may be startled by the mode in another society, as for instance English people are when they say of the Irish that they are always harping on about history. But in England, where imperial history has been favourable to the survival of buildings, statues, paintings and institutions, young citizens are daily reminded, for good and ill, of how things came to be the way they are. In Ireland, our history is just as long, but it has been interrupted by a long period of colonialism unfavourable to the development and preservation of the visual reminders one can see everywhere in England, Germany or France. Generally speaking, we are left with less that we can look at, and our institutions are mostly no more than modifications of those left behind by the imperial power, so we are driven to frequent commemorations by necessity. Commemorations, particularly in the absence of what is taken for granted in countries with a continuous history of self-government, are not in themselves evidence of an obsession with the past. In fact, they are a way of speaking about the present.[22] It is arguable that the current uncertainty in the Republic about what events of the past to celebrate and how, reflects serious uncertainty about the present and no vision for the future.

4

Stories with/without an End in View

As we have seen, any society may be expected to cherish and by ritual and commemoration re-enact or realise the self-justifying story of its own past. The dominant group within a society will attempt to make its own version of how things once were acceptable to all, in order that minorities and the dominated may then more readily accept how things are now, today. The oppressed and the dominated are likely to cherish another view of the past, if only because they are experiencing the present in a way that is less comfortable and happy than their masters probably even realise it is. But they may not: for the din made by the oppressors' story may be so loud as to have drowned out the losers' one. It may even have caused a collective amnesia among the oppressed about their past and engendered in them an under-estimation of their own value or significance in the present. This is what is described fictionally by Coetzee in his novel *Waiting for the Barbarians*, discussed in chapter 1, and is well documented in fact among women, blacks and others.

A healthy society will have the confidence and the courage to allow the memories of the oppressed and the officially censored or forgotten to be articulated—perhaps for the first time. That can only be a good thing. But a healthy society will scarcely rest at that point. It will wish to *include* the story of the deprived, the censored and the oppressed in a new way, allowing their story to judge and to modify what has been up to now the unchallenged story of the dominating group. But it will want to go on from there to allow the future hoped for by the oppressed a place in its own commemoration of the past and aspiration for the future.

Paul Lehmann, writing of 'story' in the context of revolutionary experience, has this to say:

> *The story . . . refers to the way in which one generation tells another of how the future shapes the present out of the past*; how destiny draws heritage into the human reality and meaning of experience, which is always a compound of happenings, hope and remembrance; how promise and disillusionment, celebration and suffering, joy and pain, forgiveness

and guilt, renewal and failure transfigure the human condition and are transfigured in it.[1] (Italics mine)

He goes on to suggest that revolutions are happenings of such 'depth, intensity and consequence' as to require a 'story', in this sense, 'to hold these happenings together'. They happen 'when the burden of unfreedom becomes unbearable and explodes into a new beginning, with a story all its own'.[2] Certainly since 1789 and on various occasions since, new worlds have for a time seemed to open up to the vision of those who could adjust their focus to take them in. Since 1789, as Hannah Arendt puts it, 'it has been the boundlessness of their sentiments that made revolutionaries so curiously insensitive in general to reality, and in particular to the reality of persons, whom they felt no compunction in sacrificing to their *principles*, or to the course of history or to the cause of revolution as such.'[3]

This was, of course, true of France in the slide from revolution to Reign of Terror, in Russia, in China and elsewhere. Indeed, it is a tenor of mind that has more than once stained the record of Puritan reform in the history of the Church. We live in the wake of the collapse of Stalinism and of the East European socialist experiment where persons and even large groups of persons were so often sacrificed without compunction. Fresh revelations about the secret police or labour camps or mass graves or any other of the horrific sacrifices to the cause of 'principle, the course of history or the revolution as such' are bound to make us uncertain about the validity of any appeal to the future or to 'the great end in view'. That is understandable. But those of us who prize the Judaeo-Christian tradition should keep our heads in what we may call this flight from eschatology, this flight from any future orientation. The consumerist free market economy, which is now enjoying its moment of triumph, has no end in view other than self-perpetuation.[4]

We will return to this task of telling one another 'how the future shapes the present out of the past' and how it may be seen as the specifically Christian contribution to the debate in a later chapter. Just now, we may perhaps consider what light, if any, is cast by Paul Lehmann's notion of 'story' upon the two ideologies at work in Ireland—particularly in the North of Ireland—i.e. the Protestant-unionist and the Catholic-nationalist.

Admittedly what happened in Ireland in 1912 with the Ulster gun-running and the signing of the Covenant, or in 1916 at the GPO and elsewhere, were not events to be compared in scale or consequence with what happened in France in 1789, in Russia in 1917 or in China in 1948. And certainly a strong case could be made for saying that, although the UVF gun-running to Larne preceded the foundation of the Irish

Volunteers, the UVF was a counter-revolutionary rather than a revolutionary force. But this is not the place to enter into that argument. Suffice to say here, perhaps, that both the political units which came into existence in Ireland post-1920 did so as a result of military and revolutionary or at least quasi-revolutionary activity. In both parts of Ireland, the articulate committed themselves orally and in writing to a certain vision for the future and/or set their faces against a future which they feared to contemplate. On both sides there were people who were prepared to die for their convictions, and some did.

At that time there was within the independence movement, and arguably even within unionism, a future dimension to their vision. We turn now to consider what has happened to that dimension in the period since, first with reference to various strands of Protestant-unionism, and second with reference to Catholic-nationalism.

(a) Protestant-unionists and the future

The story is that of the garrison or the planter or the political refugee from Scotland or the true Christians or the migrant workers, and how they have maintained themselves. The story carries within it a certain pride in achievement, a touch of racial superiority, some guilt, some jealousy. Whether the picture it gives is accurate or not, as an account of the *past* it is clear and unambiguous.

But when we turn to the future as envisioned by these same people, it is not simply that the future has become problematic or uncertain for the unionist people. The future is always that! Rather it is that the future scarcely figures at all in any realistic way. Indeed, it is one of the saddest characteristics today of a people who regard themselves as a provident, hard-headed no-nonsense crowd, that they seem to entertain no very clear vision for the future. Of course, garrison communities, such as the Protestant community in the North of Ireland vestigially is, do survive after their period of usefulness in that role is over. Unless they can find some new role or some fresh vision, they are condemned to a twilight world, some of them even mumbling *sotto voce* that of course some day there probably will be a united Ireland, but assuming that it will not come till after their day.

However that may be, it is an observable fact that when a dominant group sense themselves to be cornered in a historical *cul-de-sac*, it becomes impossible for them to conceive a future in which they do not dominate. Inevitably, under such circumstances, conspiracy theories flourish. An amalgam of more or less improbable allies are seen to be involved in a well-laid plot to subvert the State, whether it be Protestant Ulster, white

South Africa or the State of Israel. In the 'conspiracy' against 'Ulster', Rome, London, Moscow and the EC have been seen as working in concert with Dublin to undermine that Protestantism of which 'Ulster' is of course 'the last bastion'. Ian Paisley has frequently seen significance in the fact that the EC was brought into being by an instrument known as the Treaty of Rome! More sober critics of the EC may be surprised to learn from Dr Paisley that the preponderance of Roman Catholics within it is one of the most telling arguments against the EC.

On the Sunday before the European Parliament elections of 1984, Paisley is reported to have delivered a sermon entitled 'The Woman rides the Beast: a remarkable prophetic fulfilment'.[5] The woman on the commemorative stamp produced by the British Post Office in that year was intended to represent Europa being carried off by Zeus in the form of a bull. But she was recognised by Dr Paisley as none other than 'the woman of Babylon, the bride of the Antichrist, the Church of Rome herself'. He drew attention to the fact that the fourth great beast seen in his vision by Daniel had ten horns and, perhaps a little arbitrarily, identified the Common Market as the beginning of the ten-horned beast which will be smashed by the stone of Christ at the end of all things. Turning to Revelation 17 he found another beast, this time mounted by a woman 'a great whore . . . full of abomination and filthiness of her fornication . . . and drunken with the blood of the saints and with the blood of the martyrs of Jesus'. By the end of that evening no listener could have failed to conclude that the Catholic Church was the woman 'riding on the beast today', or go away without a chilling sense of what that was likely to mean for Protestant Ulster.

William McGrath, who in 1966 founded *Tara*, a loyalist paramilitary group, was apparently also a British Israelite. According to British Israelites in the north of Ireland, the British monarchy is descended from King David through a Jewish princess who reached these western islands, and came ashore like William of Orange at Carrickfergus, Co. Antrim. According to this theory, Ireland was originally a Protestant country and will be so again. During the mid-60s McGrath was organising what became known as *Tara* into ten-men platoons to face a 'doomsday' situation, a loyalist Armageddon which would be brought on by a Catholic republican rebellion. August 1969 was seen by many *Tara* members as that moment. The bizarre nature of their views and the smallness of their numbers should not necessarily lead us to imagine that they were not influential in Orange, Church and Unionist Party circles. They were.[6]

Vincent Crapanzano documents similar phenomena in another dominant grouping—the whites of contemporary South Africa.[7] There too, future hope has been collapsed into apocalypticism. The sense of being trapped in a historical *cul-de-sac* encourages the notion that the end is at hand. Such an idea is perhaps never far from the surface of consciousness for people who have lived always with a sense of enemies without and traitors within, ready at any moment to annihilate them. For such people it is easy to entertain the possibility that a conflict of cosmic proportions is to be fought out on the very homeland of those who more steadfastly than any others believe themselves to have maintained the truth or held aloft the torch of truth.

This ultimate catastrophe is often seen as having been precipitated by busybodies from outside, well-meaning or sinister, who have insisted on interfering in a situation they cannot possibly understand because it is *sui generis.* If they had not done so, all would have been well, it is claimed. In the case of the North of Ireland it is, of course, arguable that things were going to change and would have, even if there had been no civil rights movement at the end of the sixties. Liberal unionists today often refer to the sixties with nostalgia as to the lost days of normality when change could have evolved without social dislocation and disruption. In the mid-sixties, while rougher elements were still chanting 'No surrender! Not an inch!' liberals were with some confidence prepared to say that change, even in the North of Ireland, is of the essence of human existence, though of course with the proviso that it must be orderly. In fact, they almost certainly saw themselves as the ones to monitor that change. After 5 October 1968 however it was clear that change, if it came, must be the response to the demands of others. As a result, most liberals ran for cover sooner or later. But at least today the liberal will concede what the hard-liner may still deny i.e. that it is not possible to go back to 1967. But neither liberals nor hard-liners seem to have any vision of what exactly should lie ahead, or what kind of future we should be aiming for.

When all that has been said, it should also be remembered that the Protestants of the North-East did, for a time in their history, have a sense of being in the van of progress. A well-known Orange banner portrays Queen Victoria on her throne handing a Bible to a kneeling Indian prince. It has the superscription 'The secret of England's greatness.' The view from the crest of the wave of a Christian Empire was good, and it was one which neither a Home Ruler like the Rev. J.B. Armour of Ballymoney[8] nor Arthur Griffith himself[9] had any wish to lose. But the Irish unionist of the turn of the century could and did feel gratified (a) with honorary membership of a master race which claimed a sort of moral superiority over so many of the peoples of the world, including the other imperial powers, and (b) that he was involved in the wave of progress of which the early industrialisation of Ulster, the linen mills, the largest rope-works in the world and the Queen's Island were significant expressions close to home.

It seemed that Ulster belonged to the great new industrial future. Not even the housing or the poverty, the tuberculosis and the rickets that went with that industrialisation could quite blot out a certain pride—even among the workers themselves—in that achievement. This achievement compared favourably in the minds of those who were in a position to make the comparison and in the imaginations of those who were not, with the poverty and stagnation of 'the South' which later in 1921, according to this view, was to 'cut itself off' from the march of empire.

What was not immediately clear to all in 1921 or for a while thereafter, was that empire was no longer marching. It was stumbling to a standstill, even if it was to be succeeded by new modes of exploitation on the part of the countries of Europe and North America. Indeed, these new modes of exploitation and the neo-colonialist policies developed in the 1950s and 1960s, increasingly exposed Northern Ireland as an anachronism—no longer useful and indeed potentially embarrassing to those whose interests it had been created to protect. The more alert of the unionist leaders recognised this, and called on the British government again and again to renew its pledges to 'the people of Ulster'.

The ecumenical movement, particularly in the years after the Roman Catholic Church joined that movement during the Second Vatican Council, combined as it was in the minds of many loyalists in the North of Ireland with the wooing of Dublin by London prior to proposed simultaneous application for membership of the EC, yet again awakened that siege mentality of the unionist which is never far from the surface. Cries of 'Lundy!' and 'Traitor!' were shouted at successive unionist leaders. The renewed insecurity of unionist people, religious and political, actually made Ian Paisley into a significant force, and indeed he is as much a symptom of that insecurity as he is a protagonist.

Beginning in the O'Neill years (1963–69) there was among Ulster unionists an increasing sense of being cold-shouldered or simply being put on a par with those whom they had always, in the pursuance of their function, kept at a distance or even despised. The sense of being abandoned by London was more than a mere blow to self-esteem. It was devastating: and it was most traumatically so for the less privileged among the unionist population who had for so long nursed a sense that they were bearing the burden and heat of the day while others sat at ease or, if things got too hot, could hope to make good their escape. Even those who are talking today, often seem to have no clear vision of the future. And it is hard to imagine how they could develop one, since they do not really trust British governments, of either party, any more. What they do appear to be recognising is that simply to go on saying 'no' will not allow them to salvage anything at all from the wreckage. In all this, one thing is clear—the future of inevitable progress toward which their forebears in 1912 assumed they were moving, has been pulled away like a rug.

Of course, it would be misleading to suggest that all, or even most unionists are attracted by the apocalypticism we have described. Side by side with those who are, we find 'liberal' unionists who live in and for the present only, without entertaining an eschatological vision. They are benevolent people who quite honestly wish for better relations with their Catholic neighbours. They are almost exclusively middle class and the neighbours they have in mind are too, of course. They vote for the more liberal candidates put up in certain constituencies by the Official Unionists and for the Alliance Party candidates. The most earnest of them may even belong to reconciliation groups like the Irish Association or Corrymeela. The less earnest simply hope to 'bring reasonable Catholics round' and so maintain something very like what was once the *status quo* by a minor adjustment here and a little sharing there. Such people tend to regard too great an interest in the past as an unhealthy preoccupation, a 'harking back', a 'harping' on what is over and done with and, as such, fundamentally unsophisticated. For their part, they are concerned with the business of 'living here and now', and they pride themselves on what is called 'taking people as you find them'. But what they run the risk of overlooking is that how and where you find people is not altogether haphazard: individuals and groups are in particular social and economic positions and have particular dispositions mostly for identifiable *historical* reasons.

The most unthinking or at any rate, uncaring of this group have cut themselves off emotionally from the turmoil around them. They are to be seen driving past it on the motorway from the house in Bangor or Holywood to the office in Belfast and home again at night. These, rather than the working class unionists, are the ones who affect to be 'British'—less one suspects, because of any political or emotional identification with Britain, than because they wish by that identification to distance themselves from a conflict which they do not readily concede they have any part in or bear any responsibility for. The house in Bangor could as well be in

Hampstead or the outskirts of Manchester. They are the 'coasters' John Hewitt wrote of in 1969:

> You coasted along . . . .
> You even had a friend or two of the other sort,
> coasting too: your ways parallel.
> Your children and theirs seldom met, though,
> being at different schools.
> You visited each other, decent folk with a sense
> of humour. Introduced, even, to
> one of their clergy. And then you smiled
> in the look-glass, admiring, a
> little moved by your broadmindedness . . .
> You always voted, but never
> put a sticker on the car;
> a card in the window
> would not have been seen from the street . . .
> . . . Now the fever is high and raging;
> Who would have guessed it, coasting along?
> The cloud of infection hangs over the city,
> a quick change of wind, and it
> might spill over the leafy suburbs.
> You coasted too long.[10]

In another poem, *The Glens*, Hewitt contemplates the people of the Antrim glens among whom he and his wife spent a lot of time in their holiday home at Cushendall. The people of the glens represent for him the native population of Ireland who were not shifted or transplanted in the re-apportionments of land in the seventeenth and subsequent centuries, who have a tacit sense of continuity he cannot share, though he can appreciate. He says of them:

> I know their savage history of wrong
> and would at moments lend an eager voice,
> if voice avail, to set that tally straight.[11]

There is a disarming honesty in this. He knows their history: he confesses that 'at moments', rather than consistently, he really would like to speak on their behalf, and yet there is in the last line cited the acknowledgment that words are not likely to change anything very much. The irony is that Hewitt's very sensitivity and awareness came close to inhibiting practical action in him as effectively as ever it did in the anti-intellectual Philistine 'coasters' he castigates. He could, however, with scrupulous honesty affirm the 'others', and did. He could affirm

Ireland from the peculiar perspective of the Ulster Protestant of remote Scottish origins, and out of that he mines a certain tentative vision for the future which is all the more precious for being so rare:

> This is my home and country. Later on
> perhaps I'll find this nation is my own,
> but here and now it is enough to love
> this faulted ledge, this map of cloud above,
> and the great sea that beats against the west
> to swamp the sun.[12]

Hewitt's celebration of 'the faulted ledge' was, of course, his contribution and it was a great one, largely ignored at the time and never given political effect. But the tentative vision ('later on/perhaps . . . ') has its roots in something wholesome—an inclusive, not an exclusive vision.

John Hewitt's own life was that of the artist peripheralised by the Belfast bourgeoisie. He was a teacher, if you like, living on the edge of a society the official education system of which failed by and large to meet the predicament which he was trying to confront. In educational circles there was generally a belief that encounter with the 'great minds of civilisation' would itself produce magnanimity. Sometimes, it did—particularly among those who left Northern Ireland, never to return. But most often it did not: and certainly what was learned in the classroom impinged little on the conduct of social and political life.

Queen's University, in spite of its extraordinary achievements particularly in the fields of medicine, engineering and architecture, must bear a weight of blame in this regard. The fact that a number of the young activists of the civil rights movement from 1968 onwards were university students in no way diminishes the case against Queen's. In any case, their education was due largely to the educational reforms put through the British parliament by the Labour government of 1945–51 and extended in due course to Northern Ireland, in spite of the misgivings and reluctance of many unionists. By the 1960s the results of free secondary education and university grants were beginning to be evident. Young members of the Catholic community were anxious to insist on the rights and opportunities for which their education seemed to them to have been preparing them. Unionists had for long held that Ulster was British; the civil rights movement was determined to insist on seeing if that slogan could be cashed in terms of equal rights for all.

It is an unfortunate fact of Northern life that, on the whole, Queen's had not been preparing itself or its students over the preceding decades for this eventuality. Its medical faculty was, of course, almost entirely 'home-grown' but in arts, where discussion of issues should normally thrive, the personnel was largely imported. As might have been expected in a rapidly-growing university in a place like Belfast, a high proportion of posts were filled by young people from Britain who, when opportunity knocked, went home again having served their apprenticeship in Queen's. The first president of Queen's University, Dr Hamilton, who survived the change from college to university, was the last Irishman to serve in that capacity for more than two generations. His successors, many of them very distinguished men, stayed for a limited term, picked up a knighthood and returned to the no doubt more congenial world of the Oxbridge college or the BBC. Liberal native academics like R.M. Henry, professor of Greek and brother of Paul Henry the painter, were soon outnumbered in the years after 1908 when Queen's became an independent university, by scholars whose commitment to the domestic situation was minimal. One or two 'went native', like Douglas Savory, who actually became a unionist MP. A majority of the staff had no inclination at all to learn what was going on only a few hundred yards away, in Sandy Row or on the Falls Road. To them, in some ways quite understandably, it all appeared as tribalism or a tiresome replay of the religious wars of the seventeenth century. They did not hesitate to imply or even say explicitly to their students that the only sophisticated attitude to adopt towards the society they were supposed to serve was one of bemused detachment. It probably seemed that the best service they could render their students who were the products of that society was to call them out of it. The graduates of Queen's soon learned in any case that, if they stayed in the North of Ireland, society was so ordered that they had to compete—not with all, but only with a proportion of their peers. This gave them a strong motivation for not subjecting the society to too close a scrutiny in the meantime. Understandably, they came to hope that it would all last at least for their time. They did not look ahead too far.

Of recent times there has grown up among liberal unionists a vague sense that the EC has changed everything. The probability that national frontiers are not going to be as significant as once they were, should take some of the heat out of the debate in Ireland, it is argued. They perceive also, with reference to 'the South' that, whatever else about it, it is not a breeding ground for what is called in such circles 'the loony left'. So even if some accommodation with the Republic had to be sought in the future, at least important things like profits and property would be safe enough. Considerations of this sort take the future into account, but they clearly belong to the sphere of reflection on a remote future.

Liberal unionists are for the most part people whose educational opportunities have been such as to offer them at least the possibility of escaping from the North of Ireland to some other part of the world—a possibility less readily available to the poor and the unskilled. This thought no doubt serves to diminish their sense of urgency in tackling the problem. Their equivalent in South Africa would be the English-speaking whites, who feel culturally and linguistically freer to escape than their Afrikaans-speaking neighbours. The English South Africans apparently lack the emotional and racial cohesiveness of the Afrikaners, and tend to refer to England or Britain as 'home', though not infrequently a visit 'home' turns out to be a disappointment and the occasion of the shattering of long-held illusions. Wise-crackers suggest that PFP stands, not for Progressive Federal Party, but for passport for Perth! The decision to escape is understandable, but it does represent failure to be able to visualise any future in South Africa or in Northern Ireland differing from the past.

Vincent Crapanzano noted a significant difference as between the representatives of the English and Afrikaans-speaking whites in response to his introducing himself as an American social anthropologist studying the nature of stereotyping in South Africa. Afrikaners, he says, 'began, without exception, to recount their history, the way they had been wronged by the English and how they were misunderstood to-day . . . Once the Afrikaners had presented themselves and their victimization, they were almost always eager to participate in my research.'[13] The English responded quite differently: of them he says that 'they usually interrupted my introduction, cast themselves as informed colleagues, and began to describe the Afrikaners', often in a patronising way, dismissive and hostile to the Afrikaans language movement which symbolises for them their own loss of political power and excites in them from time to time a worry about their own identity. As early as 1909, Patrick Duncan, quoted by Crapanzano, pin-pointed the distinction this way:

> The Boers, whatever their differences may be, are in the last resort solidly fenced round by national and racial feelings. The others have about as much cohesive principle as chaff on a windy day.[14]

Crapanzano himself contrasts the 'vague communion' of the English on the one hand with the 'monolithic nationalism' of the Afrikaners on the other, and adds 'The English do not have a composed tradition, a secure world picture and an articulate ideology.'[15]

He also notes (p.36ff) that the identity of the English was always more 'international' than that of the Afrikaners but that, within South Africa itself, since the Union they have had to come to terms increasingly and in 1948 traumatically with minority status even within the 'enfranchised nation'. They have been variously described as living in 'complacent horror' (Crapanzano) and in 'comfortable political suffocation'. The word 'comfortable' here is particularly important, underlining as it does the fact that English South Africans are beneficiaries of a system which, up to a point only, they oppose. Crapanzano (p.37) notes that just as the Afrikaners have measured themselves against the English, so too without admitting it the English respond to the Afrikaners.

Relations between the mass of unionist people in the north of Ireland and the liberal or detached unionists I have been trying to describe have something of the same character as those between Afrikaners and English South Africans. Middle class Protestants in the North of Ireland, like English South Africans who blame it all on those 'mad Transvaalers', like to make a scapegoat of Protestant paramilitaries, of bigoted Orangemen or personally of Ian Paisley. Of course, they may also be half envious of the Orangemen and loyalists whom they otherwise despise, but who are so securely fenced round by religious, national and even racial feelings, which contrast so starkly with their own sense of isolation and deracination.

However, it should be added that social encounter with English South Africans and with detached comfortable unionists is normally a pleasant experience. The objective and well-educated observer will find plenty to talk to them about and, even if the political situation is introduced into the conversation, it may even be calmly discussed—certainly with a stranger. In either case, however, the emotional temperature may rise suddenly and unpredictably. In the case of the Ulster unionists this has to do with a recognition deep down that they are beneficiaries of a system which they do not always care for but do not really want to tinker with. It also has to do with the strain imposed upon people by an extended period of stressful waiting for the unknown to happen. People in the North of Ireland still sometimes speak of a return to normality, but very few liberals have any clear picture of what the constituents of normality would be.

(b) Catholic-nationalists and the future

As we shall see later, anyone examining the future orientation or vision of the non-unionist population must differentiate the Catholic-nationalist tradition on the one hand from the republican one on the other. It has been the positive contribution of Conor Cruise O'Brien that he has shown us the extent to which these have interwoven or, to change the metaphor, the ways in which the first has used the second as a stalking horse.[16] But to acknowledge the truth of that insight is not to concede that these two traditions have merged into one another. Certainly it would be our contention that whereas the Catholic-nationalist tradition today has no particular aim in view, the republican tradition, as represented by the men and women of the 1790s has.

Commentators on the period post-1920 have pointed out the unattractive results in the twenty-six counties of a partly successful revolution being followed by a partly successful counter-revolution. Partition in 1922 had the effect of producing a state with a population, at that time, 90 per cent Roman Catholic. The temptation to set up a Catholic state was clearly very strong and, in a number of ways, that is what emerged. That the temptation was resisted at all is more remarkable than the succumbing.

Whatever about that, the middle class government of the Free State and later the Fianna Fáil establishment found themselves moving further and further away from their origins in insurrection. Almost from the beginning, Free State ministers found themselves defending the State with a ruthlessness which matched Dublin Castle at its most draconian, while those who entered Dáil Éireann in 1932 as a 'slightly constitutional' party were not long before they produced a new constitution which they defended with every means to hand and by recourse to the emergency powers which they made available to themselves. Both Cumann na nGaedheal and Fianna Fáil, as heirs of the old Sinn Féin, were committed to the 1916 Proclamation and to the aims of the insurgents. Both claimed to revere the Democratic Programme of the First Dáil. The first election manifesto of Fianna Fáil echoes that Democratic Programme.

As long as Éamon de Valera was leading the party, it can be said to have been driven on by the vision of an Ireland united and able to speak its own language, an Ireland in which poverty would be eliminated and in which there would be equality of opportunity for all. It is not the place here to rehearse the ways in which they may have betrayed these visions or wag the head over the day-to-day policies they pursued which in fact made those goals impossible of achievement. Suffice to say that, for all that a bloody civil war was fought over the form of the State and its relationship to the British crown, these goals were not attained and today one may take the liberty of doubting whether there is a general will to reach them.

In the end of the day it was not the State and the national objectives but the Church which provided the social cement which held the community together. People who, under the British administration had sat easily to the State and its laws, continued to do so after independence—giving rise to the Irish antinomianism which foreign visitors have found so entertaining and quaint. Obedience to the Church was, on the whole, given more readily, and it is only recently that even a significant minority have sat as easily to the regulations and expected practices of the Church as they have always done to those of the State.

The transcendent social significance of the Church was to be seen everywhere in the early decades of the State; but it was symbolically realised in 1932 when de Valera and Cosgrave went together to meet the Papal Legate at Dún Laoire at the opening of the Eucharistic Congress and were photographed standing one on either side of him. Many at the time were touched to see men stand together with the personal envoy of the Vicar of Christ and prepare themselves to commemorate the coming of Patrick in 432 who, a few short years before, had been locked in the bitterest of armed conflicts. Looking back on it now we may still share that emotion, but note also that the institutional Church was the common denominator—the same Church whose bishops excommunicated republicans in that conflict. We may note, as Northern Protestants did at the time, what was then and was for long afterwards to remain the most important force in Irish life.

During the last thirty years, but especially since 1969, many goals have been tacitly revised, and hitherto unquestioned aspirations have at least been modified—but often without open or frank debate. The official line continues to be that we seek unity and intend to restore the Irish language and prize neutrality as a central plank of foreign policy.

Young people in the Republic today certainly see something anomalous in the behaviour of elders who even half-heartedly salute the men and women of 1916 and then pursue the most conservative monetarist policies, who speak of our 'traditional' neutrality and at the same time bind us into the Western military alliance, who commend Pearse's essay 'The Murder Machine' but pursue social policies that in fact put first-class education beyond the reach of all but the affluent. Some are appalled, but more, unfortunately, are coming to share the cynicism of their elders.

It is highly undesirable continually to be appealing to ideals and pretending to goals which, in practice, you have turned your back on. But this is what has happened. We constantly confuse people at home and well-wishers abroad. We leave them unsure at any given time as to whether we mean what we say when we speak of for instance the unity of Ireland, or whether we are just brushing down and toying with a theoretical ideal. Because we have no future vision and no plans in terms of which to shape the present we have engaged in a programme of repudiating a past in which a future vision was cherished, and simply 'getting on with the business of living'. The comparative youth of many of our aspirant entrepreneurs and leaders who are doing just that should not blind anyone to the cynicism of it, or to its sterility.

The attraction of Sinn Féin and the INLA for many other young people lies in the fact that they appear to operate out of loyalty to a vision of the future. So compelling is their vision that they have been able to ask for and to get extraordinary sacrifices from the young—their hunger-strikers, their volunteers. To those outside their movements, however, it often appears that (to quote Hannah Arendt again) they have become 'curiously insensitive to reality in general and to the reality of persons in particular', whom they feel 'no compunctions in sacrificing to their "principles" or to the cause of history or to the cause of revolution as such'.[17] When we begin to rake the ashes in these cases to see what went wrong, we are probably mistaken to conclude that they are greater sinners than any others, or more bloodthirsty. It may be that paramilitary organisations attract persons of sadistic or masochistic tendency, but it would need to be proved. What has happened is that quite ordinary people have been conditioned in the way Frantz Fanon describes to do what they would not 'normally' do, under the influence of a false or historically displaced model.[18] That is to say, in the case of the Provos, their goal of a self-sufficient nation State is being fought for today in terms of a model forged for the nineteenth-century and early twentieth-century struggle against imperialism. It may well be that the specifics of their goal are awry, but certainly their blunt mechanical application of the past to the current situation in Ireland involves them in a tragic misunderstanding of the present. It also involves them in a total misunderstanding of the role of their unionist fellow-citizens in the conflict. Their assassination of the 'agents of the British war machine' which a majority of fellow-citizens see simply as killing Protestants, prevents them gaining the credibility which some, at any rate, of the rest of what they have to say may possibly deserve.

The Provos must bear a great weight of blame for failing to recognise that the movement which in their case they call the movement of liberation, takes place in a constantly changing environment. People have changed since 1912: the role of the unionists has been altered in the kinds of ways we have been discussing. The changed role doesn't necessarily make unionists more attractive people, but it does fortify the requirement to understand what is happening to them and to sensitise oneself to their predicament and the kinds of fears and hopes they have for their children. However that may be, the Provos cannot go on imagining it is the lion of the British Empire they are fighting. They are right to recognise that there is an enemy, but they have made a tragic mistake in identifying who the enemy is.

In summary then, it may be said of Sinn Féin and the IRA that they are tragically mistaken at two levels. First, they are operating as though they were leading a struggle against nineteenth- or early twentieth-century imperialism, and so every day they misunderstand who the enemy is. Secondly, the aim they have in view is confused by the fact that the self-sufficient nation State which they appear to be fighting for is no longer a practicable or even, in the view of most, a desirable possibility. The goal they set before their volunteers has the merit of clarity, but it belongs to a world that is gone.

5

Identifying the Enemy

The fact that every story has a point and that the story of every group has a function has been discussed at length in chapters 1 and 2. One of the effects of that in the Irish situation as a whole, and in Northern Ireland in particular, is that young people can grow up living physically very close to one another, but knowing almost nothing of how things appear when they are looked at from the other side of the fence. This is the problem which the Programme for Mutual Understanding is addressing.[1] How successful that programme can be in a divided primary and secondary school system is open to question, but it deserves to succeed. Social and cultural division has also been addressed with some success over recent decades by the Corrymeela Community and others who bring groups of people from, say, the Falls Road and the Shankill together in Ballycastle and allow them in fresh surroundings to say how it all seems to them and their friends.

Hearing how it appears to the others can be a deeply disturbing experience, as appears for instance in the account given by a man who in 1955 at the age of twenty-two went to an Irish summer college in Co. Donegal. He had been brought up in the Protestant middle class in Northern Ireland, and needless to say, had not had the opportunity of acquiring a knowledge of Irish. His arrival went unnoticed but, as time passed, and he did not participate in the acts of worship of the other students, the truth dawned upon them that there was a Protestant in their company. After everybody had mentally checked on what sort of things they might conceivably have said up to that point, all was well. The young man turned out at least not to be a unionist—which was strange, right enough, but a great relief all round. But during those days before the penny dropped, that young man heard again and again with a candour and a passion that devastated him, how it felt to be his age and a Catholic, growing up in Northern Ireland. He had had Catholic friends all his life, played with them, gone fishing together. But they had not ever spoken so unguardedly or with such pent-up resentment or bitterness. Perhaps they had not felt it—he could not tell. No doubt they too, once on the safe side of the border would have sung the national anthem after the raising of the tricolour with the same single-minded passion as the students at the Irish College.

What disturbed that young man so profoundly was not alone that he was hearing the resentment of others expressed for the first time openly and uninhibitedly, but that he also knew what he could not say in response—i.e. that some, at least, of the accusations that were being hurled and assumptions that were being made were unfair or inaccurately based. Any member of a dominant group coming up against the uninhibited expression of the resentment of the oppressed for the first time will be shocked in this way. Only after a period of reflection will it be possible calmly to recognise that those who have been confined or hurt by oppression and discrimination are not likely to arrive easily or immediately at a dispassionate analysis of their circumstances or at a scrupulously fair delineation of their oppressors. And this will apply as readily to those who endured fifty years of unionist rule in the North of Ireland as, say, to women who in most parts of the world for the greater part of human history have endured the indignities imposed on them in patriarchal society.

After the dominant group, which normally controls the media of communication and education, has subjected the identity of the oppressed to assault, ridicule or battery over a period of time, the response of those under attack is unlikely to be cool or balanced at all times. Iain Crichton Smith, the Scottish Gaelic poet, in one of his English poems has already been quoted as saying: 'The anthology of the other is a book I had not reckoned with.'[2] Part of what the member of the dominant group, who first hears and takes in the story of the dominated people, will not have reckoned with is their tone of voice and, from his/her point of view, their exaggerations, unfairness and bitterness. But it is unreasonable to expect that it should be otherwise. For the 'strident' tone of the response is only the obverse of the grotesque misrepresentations of the oppressed in the oppressors' account of them. Too long a time of suffering, too long a sacrifice may 'make a stone of the heart'. If by any chance it produces anything as compassionate and beautiful as, say, the spirituals of the American blacks, that is just an unexpected bonus. It will take time and grace in the members of the dominating group to recognise themselves in the distorting mirror held up to them so insistently. But it must be done.

Once the period of discrimination or the colonial era comes to an end there is often an extended period of what Michael Farrell in his novel

Thy Tears might cease called 'slave-heartedness'. The version of events, the story as told by the dominant people or colonial power, lives on in the minds of those they formerly dominated. It inhibits the growth of self-esteem or confidence and self-reliance. Long after the colonial period in Ireland had passed, there has survived in many quarters a childish reliance on a system of patronage—now stemming from TDs and local councillors—rather than an insistence on democratic rights. No doubt linked to this is what looks like a lack of moral courage which *ignores* what those in authority demand, rather than argue the point openly. This is the 'slave-heartedness' of those who exchange one tyranny for another, and do it willingly because their self-respect has over centuries been seriously diminished.

There is a further point about listening to the tale of the losers, the oppressed or those discriminated against. The members of the dominant group are so blinded by their own version of how things are and by their deep fear that any change is probably a change for the worse, that they find it very difficult actually to hear what the others are saying or understand clearly what they are talking about. So it was, in the early days of the Northern Ireland Civil Rights Association in the late sixties and early seventies. When unionists heard the call for 'one man (sic!) one vote!' they pointed out that plural voting only applied in local elections. When that anomaly was abolished, further demands *vis à vis* the B-Specials or discrimination in jobs and housing were made. Bit by bit, something was done to remove those grievances too, but the trouble continued and the discontent persisted. Unionists complained that it was impossible to please some people and that, in any case, the alleged grievances were only a smoke-screen. 'What these people really want is to pull down the state of Northern Ireland and take us into the Free State', as one Orange speaker put it in the mid-seventies. No doubt he expressed the suspicions of many others. By the mid-seventies, of course, the Provisional IRA had moved on to the offensive with a bombing campaign which was killing hundreds of people and had put the unionist and loyalist population into a defensive position. They were now the oppressed and, particularly within the 'murder triangle' of South Ulster, isolated and afraid.

Under such circumstances it has become more, not less, difficult for unionists to understand how, if at all, they can be said to have offended. Their experience is not unlike that of Mendel, one of the Jewish guerrilla group in Poland in Primo Levi's novel, *If not now, when*? Mendel is questioned about the failure of a fellow-guerrilla whom he no longer cares for, to turn up to work that morning. He answers that he is not responsible for Leonid, his fellow-guerrilla—in words that he suddenly realises are an echo of Cain's when asked by the Lord about the whereabouts of his brother Abel. He quickly dismisses the idea that he is Leonid's brother, or even his keeper. 'Of course, he was not his keeper, and still less had he shed Leonid's blood. He hadn't killed him in the field. And yet the itch persisted: maybe this is how it is; maybe each of us is Cain to some Abel, and slays him in the field without knowing it, through the things he does to him, the things he says to him, and the things he should say to him and doesn't.'[3]

The bewilderment of those who are constantly being told that they have wronged others, who know it is true but no longer know what to do about it, often issues in the search for a scapegoat—someone to blame. The conviction grows in them that, if this or that group or person were removed from the situation or punished, all would be well.

Those who either exercise power they have no right to like the South African regime, or exercise more or less legitimate power improperly like the unionists from 1920 to the mid-1970s, are rarely squeamish in their identification of 'trouble-makers', or in selecting the methods they will use to deal with them. Sometimes those in power will swing bewilderingly between reliance on a military solution and reliance on a political one; the history of Britain's involvement in Northern Ireland over the past twenty years is a case in point. Successive British administrations over this period have rarely strayed far from the assumption that military or 'security' considerations should take precedence over all others. Mrs Thatcher's government, for all its commitment to the Anglo-Irish Agreement, was obsessed by security. The paramilitaries continue still to be seen by London governments as the root of the disease rather than as the alarming symptom of a disease somewhere near the real root of which is their own stubborn political neo-colonialist presence in this island—a presence which must necessarily from time to time be defended militarily, and has been.

British governments may well have diagnosed wrongly or even perversely, and accordingly prescribed wrongly, thereby causing over the decades—not to say centuries—so much unnecessary suffering. But they are not alone. Ever since the Provisional IRA came into being at first as a defensive response to the pogrom of 1970 and the so-called 'rape of the Falls', they have worked within the understanding that what they are resisting is the British Empire in its ultimate death-throes. It is true that 'counter insurgency operations', such as had already been tried out in Cyprus and in Aden, have been used again in Ulster, and there is evidence that the army leadership sees the Northern conflict in terms of perfecting these operations for use who knows where in the future. But this should not blind anyone to the fact that relations between Britain and Ireland have altered since the end of the last century or the beginning of this. The context within which both countries must now operate happily has changed and certainly, if anything, what we have to do with now is neo-colonialism rather than the old colonialism which the IRA are set to oppose.[4]

However that may be, it is arguable that an anachronistic and catastrophic failure in consistent analysis has led the IRA to pursue their present military campaign. Gerry Adams is sufficiently sophisticated to be able to put a gloss on it, but there can be little doubt that the rank and file of the IRA have reverted to atavistic hostility, and simply identify Protestant farmers, Local Government employees, contractors and builders' labourers as agents of the 'war machine' of empire. Perhaps they need to believe that in order to do what they are doing. Those who set off the bomb at Enniskillen in 1987 identified as 'the enemy' people who were mourning or honouring young people killed in the wars of 1914–18 or 1939–45. Now it may be that in Enniskillen that day, as at other cenotaphs, there were present people who are still in love with notions of the glory of death in battle or the idea that what was involved in 1914–18 or in 1939–45 was the defense of empire and the 'Christian West'. It should be remembered that, however little they understood of it, those young lads were in fact fighting fascism and Adolf Hitler. Most of those at the cenotaph in 1987 were simply honouring their dead that day in Enniskillen. Some were no doubt also making some sort of statement directed against the paramilitary forces which were a few minutes later to blow them up. But those who set the bomb had been told by their leaders nothing of James Connolly's writing on the First World War or of how he saw the young soldiers as no more than cannon fodder to protect British, French or German business interests. Needless to say, they had told them nothing of the courageous parallel protests of John Maclean in Scotland and Liebknecht in Germany against the capitalists' war.[5] If they had told them that, then they would have left the mourners at the Enniskillen cenotaph to their melancholy commemoration. They could even have joined them in spirit. They could have seen the young men blown to pieces in the trenches as victims of the same voracious forces as executed Connolly and Liebknecht then, or perpetrated the massacre of the poor at Soweto and Kassinga or in central America to-day.

It may well be that some of those who over the years have been identified by the IRA as the 'lackeys of Empire' and cogs in the 'war machine' were themselves fairly uncompromising or even bigoted loyalists, but they were also 'Protestants or Dissenters' whom the same 'republicans' have said they aspire to draw together under 'the common name of Irishman'.[6] In the case of Enniskillen and many other bombings and 'assassinations', a narrow interpretation of the past and an exclusivist vision for the future have led to genocide in the present. The IRA has not the right to identify who shall die for the sins of this or any other people. Nor has anyone else.

A former Chief of Staff of the Provisional IRA once spoke in my hearing of 'military action' which would in fact 'raise the sectarian temperature but not', he added 'beyond the point of tolerance'. Even to say such a thing a person must assume himself or herself to be in a position to determine thermostatically the point at which fellow-citizens can take no more. It is one thing soberly to recognise the terrible fact that further casualties are inevitable in the pursuit of a resolution of our conflicts no matter what we do. It is quite another to *identify* scapegoats and, having destroyed them, expect a resolution of the conflict.

It is one thing to work for a new order of society and, on the way there or when you have arrived, recognise that others who had a substantial stake in the way things used to be will want to leave. It is quite another to begin by identifying those who must be harassed or driven out before we can establish the new order. Protestants in the border counties are left with no alternative but to think that it is the second of these courses which has been adopted. But those Protestants are, in a sense, paying the price for the policies of successive Stormont governments. They in turn had identified who was dispensable. By impeding economic development in the eastern parts of Northern Ireland, Stormont administrations made sure that emigration was much higher *per capita* from nationalist than it was from unionist areas. The motive was to counteract the higher Catholic birth rate and even, if possible, to lower the Catholic vote west of the Bann. The 'enemies of the State' were easily identified, and it was desirable that their numbers should be curtailed. Consistent with that identification an attempt was even made to abolish the child allowance for families of over three children. To its credit, the General Assembly of the Presbyterian Church which was meeting at the time, spoke out against this.[7]

Where the identification of the enemy is concerned 'Protestant' paramilitaries have been no less callous in the drawing-up of their hit lists than the IRA. There is only one important difference: they draw theirs up to maintain the *status quo* and prevent change rather than effect it, and regain ground lost by compromising politicians, liberal Churchmen and 'traitors'. Perhaps that is why they were the first to drive up to the round-abouts in certain areas of the city and indiscriminately open fire, knowing that anyone they would hit was liable to be a Catholic.

Three men, described by Sinn Féin as 'republicans', were shot dead at the end of August 1988 in a car near Drumnakilly on the road from Carrickmore to Omagh in Co. Tyrone, not far from the place where a coach-load of soldiers had been ambushed eleven days earlier. Reacting favourably to this, the Rev. Ian Paisley was reported as saying that he was glad that the shackles had been taken off the security forces. He went on: 'I hope this is not an isolated incident, but that it will be followed up by other such incidents and the IRA put down in a manner spoken about by Mrs Thatcher—"swept off the face of the earth"'. According to the same report DUP councillor, Sammy Wilson, said: 'Dead IRA men are much preferable to internment, which is a drain on the State.'[8] But even these men should not be identified as scapegoats by anyone—certainly not by ministers of Jesus Christ.

One of the most disturbing aspects of the last ten to twenty years in all parts of Ireland, but particularly poignant in the North, is the emotional withdrawal of so many middle class and well-educated people from the fray. Still sadder it is to hear them locate the source of the trouble as the 'extremists' of working class Belfast, Portadown or Derry. Some have not altogether withdrawn, of course, but maintain their membership of PACE or Co-operation North or the Irish Association, or participate in the ecumenical outreach of the parish they belong to. Many have compassion for the families of young men and women caught up in one paramilitary grouping or another but, in the end of the day, they are tempted to say that these young people must be locked up. Sad experience, and sometimes disillusionment in the wake of the failure of liberal experiments of one kind of another, can lure even rather good people into the view that there are in our society incorrigibly ignorant and bigoted persons whom we would be better without—certainly for the foreseeable future. These are people who more or less reluctantly accepted internment when it was introduced by the Stormont government in 1970 and who have always in the end accepted successive diminutions of civil liberty on the grounds that we are living through an emergency and that no innocent or decent person is going to be affected anyway because such a person, being innocent, has nothing to fear. The fact that a person's very innocence is much harder to establish on the Shankill or the Falls Road than it is on the Malone Road does not perhaps readily occur to them. Excellent people as they are, they have in effect given up on those who are less fortunately placed. They may still desperately hope that, while more strident people are either marginalised, penalised or institutionalised, the moderate middle ground will sort things out again and bring 'normality' back. But, in however genteel a form, this line of thought itself involves a form of scapegoating. Dietrich Bonhoeffer, the German pastor and professor who was deeply involved in the resistance to Hitler, speaks very directly to their situation:

> The good man too, no less than the wicked, succumbs to the same temptation to be a despiser of humankind if he withdraws in disgust, leaving his fellow-men to their own devices, and if he prefers to mind his own business rather than debase himself in public life. Of course, his contempt for mankind is more respectable and upright, but it is also more barren and ineffectual. In the face of God's becoming man, the good man's contemptuous attitude cannot be maintained, any more than can the tyrant's. The despiser of men despises what God has loved. Indeed he despises even the figure of God who has become man.[9]

Christians then take seriously, but never callously, the inevitability of further suffering and even bloodshed, no matter what direction we take in the resolution of our conflict. But they cannot ever concede the right of anyone to identify who shall suffer or whose blood be spilled, or to lay hands on any more scapegoats to be sent into the wilderness, bearing the sins of the people. The message of the Epistle to the Hebrews is that God has himself provided the scapegoat, the one who suffered outside the gate, the high priest who offered himself. We must seek no temporary relief by selecting new victims who, if removed from the scene, might cleanse the air.[10] The call of Hebrews is to quite different effect: it is the call to 'go forth to him outside the camp, bearing his reproach':

> For the bodies of those animals whose blood is brought into the sanctuary by the high priest as a sacrifice for sin are burned outside the camp. So Jesus also suffered outside the gate in order to sanctify the people through his own blood. *Therefore, let us go forth to him outside the camp, and bear the abuse he endured* (Hebrews 13: 11–13)

What that 'going forth' may come to involve for Irish Christians, what it will mean in detailed practice, has to be worked out afresh all the time as we travel along.

In this context it is perhaps worthwhile to consider for a moment what Luke has to say in speaking of the fate of Jesus. Luke has often been accused of leaning too far in a predestinating or fatalistic direction. For instance he has Peter on the day of Pentecost speaking as follows:

> This Jesus, delivered up according to the definite plan and foreknowledge of God, you crucified and killed by the hands of lawless men (Acts 2:23).

There may be some justice in the contention that this line of thought tends to turn the actors in the drama into mere puppets, but surely what it safeguards is enormously precious, i.e. the conviction that what, for want of a better word, might be called God's 'plan' is so comprehensive that no one need ever stand outside God's grace, no matter whose agents they have at one time or another unwittingly or fairly willingly, become. They may have been acting in ignorance (Acts 3:17), not recognising 'the author of life' and asking for a murderer to be granted to them instead (Acts 3:15). The Jesus of Luke certainly comes 'to cast fire upon the earth' (Luke 12:49). But this fire is clearly to be distinguished from the fire of retribution which James and John had wanted to call down upon the inhospitable Samaritan village. This reaction of theirs had immediately called forth the rebuke of their master (Luke 9:51–56). The fire of Luke 12:49 is the purifying word and act of Jesus which forces decision and will almost certainly cause dissension even within the family itself and will eventually bring about Jesus' own death. (Cf. Luke 3:16–17).

In Luke's two books, the sequence is always from revelation to repentance, not *vice versa* (Luke 15:17), and the tendency is altogether against premature retribution on our part. It even discourages attempts to identify sinners, preferring, as in Luke 13:1–5, to direct those who would do so to their own need of that radical redirection of intention which the New Testament calls *metanoia*, repentance.

The kingdom in Luke is characteristically 'among you'; it is 'making its way'. The call to the 'little flock' whose Father wills to give them the kingdom (Luke 12:32), is a call to live in anticipation of the moment when their Lord will come back from the wedding feast (Luke 13:35–36). The believing community is to be a sign of the coming kingdom, not a body of legislators or a judiciary hammering out an equitable sentencing policy. The call even to be a sign is a mark of sheer grace granted to a community which has itself sinned grievously.

Some good counsel concerning what should/should not be done, even after the 'enemy' has been clearly identified is to be found in Jesus' parable about the weeds in the fields (Matthew 13:24–31). The farmer in the story sows good seed in one of his fields but, under cover of darkness, an enemy of his comes along and sows charlock seeds among the wheat. In due course, the farmer's employees notice the weeds coming up through the wheat. They suspect the quality of the wheat seed sown, and they ask their master about it. But he has no doubts on that score: he guesses what has happened, and he says, 'An enemy has done this.' They offer to weed the field. But he forbids that, knowing as he does, that the roots of this particular weed wind themselves round those of nearby plants, with the result that it would be quite impossible to pull out the weeds without also dislodging a good part of the wheat crop as well. 'Let both grow together', he tells them, 'until the harvest; and at harvest-time I will tell the reapers, Gather the weeds first and bind them in bundles to be burned, but gather the wheat into my barn.'

This parable asserts the primacy of the good, by reference twice over to the high quality of the seeds, and of the constructive action of the farmer in sowing the field in the first place. Only secondary is the action of the enemy: his action, spectacularly mean and all as it is, has no meaning at all apart from the action of the farmer in sowing the field with wheat in the first place. So the destructive derives whatever significance it has from the constructive, not *vice versa.* This is what the believing community in Ireland is engaged to say and be a sign of, in season and out.

When the labourers express doubt about the quality of the seed sown, the farmer dismisses those doubts and invites them to share his confidence in its quality. The believing community is called to share God's 'confidence', if we may put it so, in the seed. In the eucharistic celebration we may well be understood to be sharing God's confidence in the crucified Jesus, in spite of what the enemy has done. The Eucharist may be seen as the moment in the worship of the believing community at which the crucified one invites the congregation to share with him the joy of his resurrection. Christian worship and Christian action too often assume the primacy of the darkness: in it we imagine ourselves to be called to place little lights here and there, and earnestly and even petulantly shield those candles from the draught, lest they go out. But it is the other way round: it is the light which is primary, and no darkness can put it out (John 1:5).

This parable does not, however, recommend a relativistic or a quietest stance *vis-à-vis* what the enemy has done in the field under cover of night. Before the interview with his employees is finished, the farmer indicates just how he proposes to overcome the sabotage. It is part of the genius of this parable that we never, so to speak, catch sight of the enemy—even though he has malignantly done so much damage. The labourers are certainly to be set to work to undo the sabotage, but not now and not by directing their efforts at the weeds as they stand growing in the field. If they were to act as they think best they would do more harm than good.

The believing community in Ireland is obliged to remind itself and all those outside of its ranks with whom it finds itself allied in constructive social and political work,

(1) that there is an enemy; but
(2) that the enemy is not identifiable without remainder as this or that particular individual or group, even though this one or that may very well have become the enemy's agents. In any case, his roots and ours are hopelessly tangled;
(3) that the enemy is supra-personal, and most often and most threateningly assumes *institutional* forms. The apostle Paul identifies the situation, in the following terms:
For we wrestle, not against flesh and blood [i.e. against people], but against principalities and powers, against spiritual wickedness in the heights . . . . etc. (Ephesians 6:12).

That is to say, that even though supra-personal forces and institutions may from time to time become personified in our perceptions by an Adolf Hitler or a P.W. Botha, it is not these people or even their unlovely henchmen who are the enemy, but rather the economic, social and political forces whose slaves and beneficiaries they have become. It may be that such slaves and beneficiaries will in the end be punished for the part they have played, and deserve to be. But even they must not be absolutely identified with their master.[11]

6

Expiation in Christian Perspective

In the last chapter, we alluded to the bewilderment which members of the dominating group feel when they are faced with the resentment, the accusations and the demands of those who believe they have wronged them. It is a bewilderment shared by men when women speak up, by employers who had always considered themselves benevolent when employees complain, by the Catholic hierarchy when they think they are simply stating what is for the public good and are told that they are arrogantly assuming that they always know best what the public good is, by unionists faced with the resentment of nationalists, by the establishment generally when it first comes up against the pent-up rage of young people with no work and no prospects.

Then nemesis comes upon them suddenly; payment and expiation are demanded, sometimes with terrible suddenness for debts one scarcely realised one owed. W.R. Rodgers' poem *Scapegoat* is worth re-reading in this connection:[1]

> God broke into my house last night
> With his flying squad, narks, batmen, bully-boys,
> Proctors, bailiffs, aiders and abettors
> Call them what you will, hard-mouthed, bowler-hatted.

So it begins, and then continues a few lines lower down:

> The tall figure with his obedient shadows
> Pushed past me into the light and turned
> With the accusing document; all my fears.

The 'implacably-forgiving' one bursts into the house in the middle of the night just as the man of the house is about to let the dog out and, when resistance is at its lowest, insists on a reckoning. The poem goes on:

> It seemed I had for years out of mind
> Owed him a sum of money and had paid
> Nothing. 'Lord', I said reluctantly, looking

Into his implacably forgiving face,
'I would have called it a lie, but if you
Say so, it must be so.'
I do not know —
It being a dream of sorts—I do not know
If it were His son or my son
The doomsmen laid upon the floor then,
The knife to his throat.
I saw no more. But the dog of the house
Fled howling through the open door.

Rodgers, the preacher-poet holds together two things in this poem: (1) the frightening abrupt initiative of God demanding satisfaction, 'the tall figure with his obedient shadows' and the 'accusing document: all my fears' and (2) the serious consequences of this break-in for the son thrown to the floor with a knife held to his throat while the dog, like a sort of domestic scapegoat, flies out the open door into the darkness. In his 'dream of sorts' the 'I' of the poem admits that normally he would have denied he owed a penny. Now that retribution has come, he is unclear as to whether it is God's son or his own who lies in the hallway with a knife at his throat. That uncertainty is, however, the measure both of the artistic integrity and the theological soundness of the poem. For such is the human tragedy and such is the fate of the executed Jesus that it is impossible at any given moment to say definitively or exclusively that he is only God's or only one of ours. He is ours certainly, upon whom falls the consequence of sins or, in the imagery of the poem, of 'debts' we were scarcely aware of. But he is also God's, who alone could bear so great a weight, so great an injustice. The reality and immediacy of what is happening is felt intimately and domestically by the very house dog that flies 'howling through the open door'. And, of course, on *our* children again and again *fall* the consequences in such a way that Christ is crucified again in them.

The author of the *Oresteia*, no less than the biblical writers, recognised what the researches of Freud and Marx only serve to underline, i.e. that we do suffer for wrongs we know nothing of, *for* our forebears and *with* those of them, parents and grandparents, who continue to live into our own time. The fact is that we are more intimately bound up with the ancestors than we can ever know, and more consequentially bound to and affected by contemporaries whom we will never lay eyes upon than it is always comfortable to think. Never before in human history have we been so aware of our inter-dependence as genetic, personal, psychological and economic units, linked with some in one way, with others in another, but in some way or other with all. Where this awareness develops we are perhaps a little more easily made conscious of the inevitability of the 'innocent' suffering. The fact that each one of us, and each of the groups to which we belong, is an integral part of all the rest means that the consequences, for good and ill, of what happens now or did happen once, in any other group's past may and probably will affect *us*. Whether the fathers ate sour grapes or gorged themselves on too many sweet ones, the children's teeth will certainly be affected. The idolatry of the forebear is visited by what Exodus calls the 'jealous God' 'upon the children to the third and fourth generation' but 'steadfast love' is also shown 'to thousands of those that love me and keep my commandments' (Exodus 20:4–6). Relationship with children, our own and other people's, cannot be the beautiful and awesome thing it is without its having consequences and outworkings that reach far beyond our ken into an unknowable future. And the same must surely apply to the relationship with God's self.

When things go wrong, the ones upon whom the house eventually falls may well be, to all appearances, innocent. That has been shown to be true again and again during the bombing campaign of the IRA or the outrages of the Protestant paramilitaries—the Abercorn bombing, countless street bombings, at the cenotaph in Enniskillen, the Darkley Gospel Hall, or the Dublin bombings of ten years ago.

But, perhaps more difficult for us to accept is the inevitability of further suffering and even death, even as we move *constructively* towards a *resolution* of our conflicts. Very early on in the present troubles came the pogrom of 1969, entailing attacks on 500 houses in the Crumlin Road and Lower Falls. These attacks came as a violent reaction against peaceful protest of the civil rights marches and the promise of some ameliorative action. They had, of course, been preceded by the violent reaction of the police to the peaceful protest in Derry on 5 October 1968. Even action towards progression and the amelioration of conditions is liable to provoke violent reaction in a situation which has long been controlled by institutional force.

Christians, in particular, should not have been surprised by this reaction, no matter how distressing they found it. The New Testament makes the point that even when God, God's self, is at work to remedy our predicament, it is of the nature of our predicament that it cannot alter without suffering—some of it very terrible, and some of it falling on the heads of those we would call 'innocent'. The infancy narratives in

Matthew's Gospel make this point, particularly so the story of the wise men and the story of the massacre of the Judaean children, taken as a sequence (Matthew 2:13–23). The story of the massacre of the children is closely linked to the preceding story about the Magi. It is their innocent question, 'Where is he who is born King of the Jews?' followed by their divinely-guided decision to return to their own country without going back to tell Herod where the child is to be found, which drives Herod to the extreme measure he takes against the two-year-olds and younger. The escape of the Christ-child into Egypt does not prevent the death of all those other little ones. The two stories, taken together, seem to be saying that when God begins to challenge our patterns of authority and the exercise of power, God does so from below and everyone, including even those whom we would call the 'innocent', is at least liable to get hurt in the reaction of those who hold power now.

The context of the story is set by the wise men's question already quoted, on their entry into the city, 'Where is he that is born King of the Jews?' Their study of the firmament had encouraged them to believe that fundamental changes were afoot. Following the assumptions of their time, they assumed that the star heralded the birth of a king and they assumed that such a king was to be found in Jerusalem in or near the palace of Herod. Their question and their quest have to be refined by reference to scripture, the text from Micah read out by the court theologians of the tyrant himself. Even unrefined their question was enough to disturb Herod and all Jerusalem, but refined, it drives him to violent extremes. And what Herod, as representing all those who have intrigued and murdered their way to power, immediately does is to try and stop the clock. There will be no subversive future, and to that end, he orders the murder of little children.

What he cannot live with is the nightmarish idea that out there somewhere is another kind of king exercising another kind of authority altogether, totally different from anything he had ever been, and coming up from below to challenge his own acquisition and exercise of power. Interestingly enough, the next time that Matthew tells us the whole city was disturbed is at the end of his book, when the same child, now grown to manhood, enters the city riding on a donkey—an action which symbolises a profound critique of kingship, an exercise of authority so radically critical and subversive as to call forth the confrontation which reaches its climax at Calvary.

The story of the massacre of the innocents in its starkness serves to remind us that, where God is at work, even apparently harmless bystanders may get hurt or even be mortally wounded. This is not because a ruthless God tramples everyone underfoot striding to the goal, but rather because God works, organically from below, quietly, inexorably. Those who, like Herod, have grabbed power or like Archilaeus his son have inherited and abused it, feel threatened by any change. They will never vote themselves out of power: they will defend what they have grabbed by every means at their disposal. Perhaps with this story in mind, W.H. Auden wrote in his poem *The Tyrant*, 'When he laughed, respectable senators burst with laughter/And when he cried, the little children died in the streets.'

Fastidious Christians no longer favour as an item of praise William Cowper's hymn which begins:

> There is a fountain filled with blood,
> drawn from Emmanuel's veins,
> and sinners plunged beneath that flood
> lose all their guilty stains.

They also rush over phrases in our set liturgies which seem to insist on the expiatory dimension to the death of Christ, as being a shade gruesome. But, however remote from our own liturgical experience the sacrifice of actual animals may be, animal sacrifice did give expression to the *tangible* character of human sin and alienation. For the human predicament does not arise as a result of merely mental or spiritual transgression, but of material, social and political injustice, wreaked by a humanity in the grip of supra-personal forces. The New Testament writers see God at work to establish justice in the world, and they see the consequences falling on Jesus. God has indeed 'provided for himself a lamb', in this quite unavoidable yet willingly accepted shedding of blood.

What the annual ritual of atonement at the Holy of Holies in the Jerusalem temple took seriously is also, as it were, taken for granted by the writer of the Epistle to the Hebrews. In what reads like a throw-away line he says (9:22), 'Under the law almost everything is purified with blood, and without the shedding of blood there is no forgiveness of sins.' But he recognises that, whereas the high priest in the ceremony annually repeats the ceremony 'with blood not his own' (9:25), Christ 'has appeared once for all at the end of the age to put away sin *by the sacrifice of himself* (9:26).

7

Solidarity and the Problem of Identifying

Both for those who are in the thick of it and for those who are more peripherally engaged, serious questions are raised by the demand for 'solidarity'. We have already considered examples of people who improperly pretend to be disengaged from the conflict. We have observed the attempts of some people in the twenty-six counties or of the middle class in Northern Ireland to do that with reference to the Northern conflict, or of English South Africans who shrug the whole thing off by blaming it all on 'those dreadful Transvaalers'. We have noted the side-stepping exercise of (largely conservative) groups who say of almost any conflict in the world, as soon as action on the part of the oppressed is urged, 'What about the travelling people? What about? What about . . . ? I never hear you people talk about . . . . ?' At this point we may perhaps begin to take it for granted that today we are all more involved in one another's plights than ever before. Never before in human history has it been so untrue to say to those who express interest or even take a hand in our affairs, that it is 'none of their business'. If that is so, then the question concerning what is called 'solidarity' with the oppressed and the poor, and the liberation movements through which they seek to remove the causes of their trouble, is not going to go away. It is going to become even more pressing.

We acknowledged in the last chapter that there is a problem involved in identifying who exactly represents the oppressed and who the oppressor in any particular situation. Edward Norman has derived enormous satisfaction from recording what appear to be glaring errors of judgment in this regard, as when in 1972 the Church Missionary Society hailed the personal involvement of General Amin of Uganda in a 'dispute over ecclesiastical jurisdiction' as 'a true miracle of the Holy Spirit'—to which he adds: 'Perhaps, in the circumstances, it was.'[1] One wonders whether the minister of a leading Presbyterian church in Belfast who in 1969 identified Terence O'Neill as a latter-day Josiah, the King of Judah who discovered the scroll of the law in the course of restoration work on the temple and set about the reform of Israel's religion and life, ever blushes now.

Anyone who has ever joined hands with others in what they believed at the time was a movement for liberation and emancipation, is likely afterwards to recognise that they were shoulder to shoulder with people who had alarmingly divergent agendas. But simply because the same Terence O'Neill attempted to discredit the Northern Ireland civil rights movement by implying it was the creature of republicans, communists and anarchists; simply because his Minister of Home Affairs, William Craig, as he looked at the photographs of the marches of 5 October and 16 November 1969, identified in them what he regarded as subversives; simply because there were people involved in the civil rights campaign who were all along Catholic sectarians who had never accepted the new direction which the republican movement took in the 1960s, does not mean that it was wrong to join hands with them then, even though it probably would be wrong to stand shoulder to shoulder with many of them today.

Certainly today those on the periphery who would wish to help, say, the people of West Belfast out of their misery are faced with a dangerous dilemma. It would appear that an ideological battle is being fought out for the hearts and minds of the Catholic people between Sinn Féin/the IRA and the Roman Catholic Church. The former Bishop of Down and Connor, Dr Cahal Daly,[2] was much more aware than his predecessor Dr Philbin of how much ground the Church has lost in Belfast. He recognised that it was as 'Catholics' that the people have been discriminated against, burned out and beaten up, and it is as Catholics, rather than as GAA supporters, Irish speakers or anything of the sort, that many even of the lapsed necessarily still see themselves. If the Church which they and their forebears have suffered so much for belonging to, can now offer them some of the basic material securities they crave for themselves and their children, clearly it is in their interests and the Church's that they should co-operate. The British Government has seen a political opportunity in this. As a clear response to the patronage and protection system so long and successfully run by the paramilitaries, the British Government through its agencies has made it possible for Church-related bodies to provide a high proportion of the employment that is actually available in West Belfast. The Church is turned into a counter-weight against the Provos.

The Church, as represented by Dr Cahal Daly and its other principal spokesmen, sees the results of the Provisional campaign at first hand in the grief-stricken families of the people they bury. But the Church must ask itself whether it is in the long-term interests of its fundamental mission to act as the purveyor of employment or recreational schemes on money provided directly or indirectly from government funds, themselves given with specific political and even military objectives.

It can be said that the Northern problem today, is a text-book case of how difficult it can be to know whom to support or who it is that we might wish to show solidarity with, in any effective way. Arguably today's confusion is the result of the failure of Stormont to hear and understand the call of the civil rights movement in the late sixties. The rents and rates strike called for in response to the imposition of internment was seen by unionists in terms of a threat to property and due to possible communist influence. Actually it was the only alternative protest to the military one soon to be espoused with vigour by the Provisional IRA, and should have been seen as such. But it was not, and so a great opportunity for non-violent protest was lost.

Dr Norman has seen fit to make fun of the fact that it is not the poorest or those who are suffering most cruelly whose voices we hear most clearly in South Africa or Latin America or Chile but rather those who, in his view, have been educated to a point where they can be infected with the intellectual and moral fashions of the time.[3] He suggests that we are mistaken if we listen to their voices too credulously. But Dr Norman is a history teacher, and he can hardly be surprised to find that what has been true in the past is also true today, i.e. that it is those of the people who have begun to get their heads above the water who initiate protest on their own behalf and, in the best examples, on behalf of those below them who are even worse off. So it was in France in 1789, in Ireland in the 1790s and in Russia throughout the nineteenth century. And so it was, as has so often been observed, in the 1960s in the Northern Ireland Civil Rights Association. A good deal of the impetus and energy of that movement came from the young people whom British educational policies, as extended to Northern Ireland, had now educated to the second and third level. They had the know-how and the self-confidence which their parents and grandparents had lacked. But where else would the protest have come from? It was no less valid because it came from these well-educated young people—even though their newly-acquired Trotskyite analysis did lead some groups like the People's Democracy into culpable naïvetés from time to time.

Arguably the People's Democracy were making the same error as the socialist militants make from within the international anti-apartheid movement—with the important difference, of course, that they were talking about their own country, not someone else's.[4] That is to say, they were laying down beforehand what sort of society it should be after civil rights had been granted or, perhaps, in order that civil rights *could* be granted. They were divisively breaking ranks with the campaign's primary and strictly limited aims. It is a primary requirement of solidarity movements that they do not dictate the social system or the patterns of the distribution of power beforehand. Both the Roman Catholic Church and Sinn Féin in their variously benign and sinister ways would appear to many to wish to do that.

However, the fact that it is a problematical undertaking does not ever lift from us the responsibility of showing solidarity with the poor and the oppressed and those in trouble in specific situations. Sometimes it will be difficult to identify the particular people's movement whose efforts we may confidently and conscientiously support; sometimes it will be relatively simple.

Dr Norman, like many others a good deal more liberal than he might be considered, is concerned by any expression of solidarity with the movements for liberation throughout the world which may seem to be and may actually be uncritical. No one can fault him for that. He is also wary of any crude application of Marxist or general socialist analysis to situations. It should be conceded immediately that this is a serious point and deserves to be taken seriously. Solidarity groups have at least as pressing an obligation as any others to sift evidence. But they cannot allow that to delay them indefinitely in their primary obligation to lend support to those who are actually in direct conflict with injustice, discrimination, poverty, hunger, or whatever. Solidarity groups inevitably find that things are said and done by those who are centrally involved in the struggle which they find unpalatable, incomprehensible or even distasteful. That is part of what they are asked to undergo in the struggle. They are not asked to commend the liberation movement or to condemn: they are expected to be supportive. They deny themselves the luxury of detached 'approving' or 'disapproving' this or that tactic or policy from the outside. Approval and disapproval are not appropriate stances for those who are only peripherally implicated in the plight of the oppressed. However, Ireland is so small that we are all involved, sometimes more intricately than we admit. We should therefore be in constant debate with all participants—but especially with those whose policies and tactics we most profoundly abhor.

If Christians believe (as has been suggested they should) that there are to be no more scapegoats, because God has provided a sacrificial lamb, or even more than that has entered the situation him/her self, then it follows that no one can, in principle, be left out of the 'peace process', as it is called. A very tricky problem arises here in practice. For how is one to talk to people who, like the IRA, the UVF or UFF, still believe that the conflict can be resolved in military terms, or who have identified the 'enemy' to their own satisfaction and are acting accordingly? Just how sensitive this question is has been illustrated twice in the past year or so—each time, interestingly enough, during the visit of distinguished South Africans. Both Nelson Mandela in July 1990 and Archbishop Tutu early in 1991 stated that South African experience suggested that to leave any party out of negotiations for peace is to prejudice the possibility of achieving it. Now, it is arguable that their experience in South Africa where, for seventy-five years the regime refused to speak to the representatives of the unfranchised majority is not a parallel to the Irish situation in which, say, the IRA represent so tiny a minority only. But perhaps we should not think only of numbers here. Should we perhaps consider that there will be no possibility of convincing the paramilitaries of their criminal folly until we bring them to a table somewhere? Refusal on our part to speak to them is unlikely to convince them that for us talking and negotiation are the only constructive way forward—in contrast with the way of violence *they* have chosen. Insisting that their espousal of violence makes them untouchable is very nearly true, but it is not quite. Paramilitarism is an ugly symptom of a total situation in which *everyone* is involved in some way. Those who join the paramilitaries may be wrong, but they are still part of what must be discussed, and it is arguable that they must be directly addressed.

The task of identifying the forces which are working for resolution of conflict and for progress toward democracy, participation and liberty in any given situation is a tricky one, and one which the Church will find no easier than anyone else. Nevertheless there are biblical *directions* which may prevent Christians who are involved in solidarity groups from being blown off course. And these directions are afforded by a consideration of the peculiar language used by Paul and the gospel writers.

Paul inherited from the community which he entered in Damascus and settled into at Antioch the idea of the death of Jesus as being in some way a vicarious sacrifice. But Paul is not content with the purely *vicarious* idea. In his view it is not so much a question of Christ's being *for* us or even *in place of* us: it is a question of affirming that he has become totally one with us at the most unlikely and totally compromising point of death by execution. One suspects that the gospel writers are graphically making a similar point about total identification when they tell us that Jesus died under a superscription in three languages, which there was no opportunity for him to explain or gloss or deny: 'Jesus of Nazareth, King of the Jews.'

Indeed, the point is driven home in the counterpointed usage of the term 'King of the Jews' throughout Mark 15:9,12, 16–20, reaching a climax in the mocking taunt of the chief priests and the scribes at the foot of the cross, 15:32:

> Let the Christ, the King of Israel, come down now from the cross, so that we may see and believe!'

It is characteristically part of Matthew's understanding that a kind of ambiguity is essential to total commitment and unconditional 'solidarity'. Early on in his account of Jesus' ministry, after Jesus has broken the health laws and the laws of common prudence by touching the leper (8:3), after the healing of the Roman officer's servant and Peter's mother-in-law (8:5–17), Matthew quotes Isaiah 53:4:

> This was to fulfil what was spoken by the prophet Isaiah, 'He took our infirmities and bore our diseases.'

This verse comes, of course, from the great song about the coming Suffering Servant who, it is said, 'poured out his soul to death, and was numbered with the transgressors' (Isaiah 53:12). Side by side in the passage are total commitment as far as death, potential ambiguity and irremediable misrepresentation.

And certainly this potential ambiguity is characteristic of Jesus, as presented in Matthew 12, when the Pharisees dismiss the healing of the blind and dumb demoniac by saying that it is only by Beelzebul, the prince of the demons, that the cure has been effected. To this Jesus makes two responses. First, he concedes that all such cures are problematical, not least those done by those his opponents have every faith in! So he says, 'If I cast out demons by Beelzebul, by whom then do your sons cast them out?' Then he quite simply appeals to them to make their own committed decision in faith: 'If it is by the Spirit of God that I cast out demons, then the kingdom of God has come upon you.' He and they must live, as later he is to die, with the ambiguity. That ambiguity is part of the passion which Matthew cannot disguise, and probably did not want to. In a later chapter, Jesus comforts and warns his disciples in words that no doubt hark back to chapter 12:

> The disciple is not greater than his teacher, nor the servant than his master. It is sufficient for the slave to be like his master. For, if they called the master of the house 'Beelzebul', what will they say of his servants?

Here then is a paradigm of solidarity which frontally rebukes our fastidiousness and, in the name of the crucified Jesus, calls in question our nervousness about guilt by association. If the texts we have been considering mean anything, they would seem to assert that the cross is all about guilt by association. Only the naïve will imagine that because people are oppressed or poor or systematically discriminated against, they are necessarily purified by the experience. The chances are that on the contrary, as we saw in chapter 5, they are rather damaged by it. We should therefore be amazed at the extraordinary moderation and grace at work in so many of them. In any case, it is not the duty of those who are not suffering very much at all, to assess those who are or believe themselves to be. Our task is simply that of go-between, between the God who has heard the cry of the people under their taskmasters and has come down, and the oppressed. Like Moses we are called, in spite of previous unsatisfactory efforts, to total commitment, from the burning bush to burning our boats. From the incident early on in Moses' story in which he tries to separate two Israelites who were fighting, right through the whole exodus and desert journey, Moses may be seen as struggling with the notion that these people are not worth saving anyway. His eventual failure to enter the land he had been leading them to results from his exasperation with them and his falling for the temptation to play God.

For the Christian then—and not least for Irish Christians with their fairly strongly developed self-righteousness—there is merit in keeping in the forefront of the mind, the following points:

(1) that the suffering must be addressed;
(2) that we must discover as exactly as we can who is suffering;
(3) that we must not be deflected from solidarity by *our* estimate of the sufferers' response to their situation.

It was the same Paul, on whom we have drawn so often, who wrote: 'God commends his love to us in that, while we were yet sinners, Christ died for the ungodly.' And we misread Paul badly if we reduce his notion of sinners to the level merely of transgressors, those who have committed sins of commission and omission. The 'sinners' for whom Christ died include those who may not have transgressed all that spectacularly at all, but are under 'the power of sin' (Romans 3), i.e. of those extra-personal powers of which we have already spoken, which would still hold us in their grip even if each one of us showed a 100 per cent improvement in our personal conduct sheet. And that is all of us, with whom God in Christ shows 'solidarity': and God's solidarity has to be the pattern of ours.

8
Informing Conscience

Any responsible Christian response to the challenges of our life together will inevitably involve the sensitising or, as it is often called, the informing of conscience. What this involves is to be discussed in biblical perspective in the next chapter. In this one it is proposed to survey the difficulties inherent in this process by reference to the use made of the word 'conscience' in recent years in Ireland, particularly in the course of the debates on the referenda of 1983 and 1986.

It would appear that the Roman Catholic bishops during the recent referenda in the Republic, while allowing for differences in emphasis as between individuals, took up a stance which served them then, but which can scarcely be regarded as a final resting-place. In their pastoral letter prior to the divorce amendment the hierarchy first drew a distinction between the 'political' questions and 'moral' ones.[1] 'Each legislator and each voter' they continued 'is faced with moral attitudes that affect the whole moral atmosphere of society. They can make it difficult for people to walk in the path of God's commandments.'[2] This is no doubt true; and presupposed in that pastoral is the recognition that legislation may not always correspond with Catholic, or even more generally Christian attitudes, and that Catholics often have to live with that state of affairs. The Northern bishops lead a Catholic community in which, for instance, contraception has been freely available for decades. It may be argued that this makes it 'more difficult for people' to eschew fornication and obey the Church's regulations on birth control. Clearly, however, the pastoral considers it best if temptation is not put in people's way, rather as dangerous things should be lifted out of children's reach. It did, however, concede, if that is not an unfair word, that the ultimate decision as to whether or not to provide for divorce lies with the voters and they expressed the hope that each one of them would make 'a reflective, prayerful, *conscientious* decision.'[3] (Italics mine). And indeed, not merely was the primacy of conscience emphasized by individual bishops again and again, but Dr Joseph Cassidy, then

Bishop of Clonfert, who acted as the hierarchy's spokesman even went so far, at a stage when the polls were still showing what must have looked like an alarming majority in favour of the amendment, as to say that a Catholic who did actually vote in favour would not incur 'guilt'.

Now this must surely have been reassuring for those who intended to do so anyway, but still would prefer to be, as one might say, 'in good standing' with Dr Cassidy and his colleagues. Certainly that statement of his has been cited as a major step forward towards flexibility in Church discipline and the recognition of pluralism in this part of Ireland, and it may be so. However, looked at from another point of view, it surely points up very sharply the episcopal dilemma. The bishops could scarcely do other than accord to conscience the status it has been given for centuries by moral theologians. They must also take for granted that it is the duty of the *magisterium* of the Church to inform the conscience of the faithful. They also expect that those who exercise the informed conscience will in the end make a decision in conformity with 'the commandments of God'. What was not quite clear from what Dr Cassidy had to say was whether voters, in voting, were in fact assenting to or dissenting from the commandments of God—which is clearly a matter of the utmost seriousness—or were simply voting for or against a provision which might or might not damage the moral health of society. If voters were simply exercising their judgment about something which might or might not damage society, then they were still of course engaged in a serious business, but not on so clear-cut a matter. Dr Cassidy seemed to be saying that, even though the Church has a peculiar correctness in interpreting God's will, it will not now, as once it would have, deny your right to be wrong. The 'guilt' which those who choose wrongly are to be absolved from is clearly something less significant than 'guilt' has been in traditional Christian discourse: in this context it is reduced to no more than the *loss of standing* of those who disobey the stated view and regulations of the Church.

The position which Dr Cassidy and the majority of the official spokesmen took during the divorce amendment debate (1986) was in line with the admirable sentiments expressed on behalf of the hierarchy by Dr Cahal Daly at the Forum in February 1984:

> So far as the Catholic Church and questions of public morality are concerned, the position of the Church over recent decades has been clear and consistent. We have repeatedly declared that we in no way seek to have the moral teaching of the Catholic Church become the criterion of constitutional law anywhere in Ireland, or to have the principles

> of Catholic faith enshrined in civil law. What we have claimed and what we must claim is the right to fulfil our pastoral duty, which is to alert the consciences of Catholics to the moral consequences of any piece of legislation and to its impact on the moral quality of life in society, while leaving to the legislators and to the electorate their freedom to act in accordance with their conscience.[4]

Further down Dr Daly spoke again of 'alerting the consciences of Catholics to the moral and [he added this time] *social* evils which, as experience shows, follow from certain legislative enactments. We do naturally expect these to be given mature and serious consideration by Catholics.'[5]

With very commendable modesty Dr Daly went on to deny that the bishops had ever 'suggested that the moral considerations we advance are the only relevant considerations in respect of any proposed piece of legislation. *Furthermore, we have consistently stressed the rights and responsibilities of conscience.*' He ended that section of his submission by quoting the 1973 statement of the bishops with reference to the proposed changes in the Republic's law on contraceptives. The hierarchy concluded on that occasion:

> What we are saying is that the factors we have outlined are important, and that they have tended to be overlooked in public discussion. They should be put into the balance, along with other such factors as the actual degree of inconvenience which the present law and practice cause to people of other religious persuasions and a realistic assessment as to whether a change in the law would have any significant effect at the present time on attitudes towards the unification of Ireland.[6]

The hierarchy's position, as outlined for the Forum by Dr Daly, clearly represents a significant and welcome movement towards dialogue with others. It represents a shift in aim on the part of the Church. Hitherto it had sought to control what does or does not go on to the statute book in conformity with the objective or revealed moral law. The altered stance can only be welcomed by people within and outside of the Roman Catholic Church. If we are to judge for instance from Dr Daly and Dr Cassidy's presentation of the hierarchy's position, it would appear that the bishops have retreated from that earlier authoritarian ground on to one where they simply put forward for consideration what they seriously feel will be the *probable results* of this or that proposed legislation. There is even the concession that they do not have a monopoly of insights. What they are offering people is the opportunity, in the light of the insights they do claim to have, to make up their minds, their consciences having been 'alerted' to certain considerations. That is fine: it is an invitation to the adult exercise of conscience.

Looked at from another point of view, however, there might appear to be something of an abdication of responsibility here—a flight from debate about the rightness or wrongness of divorce as such, a culpable neglect of what biblical scholarship has to say about the view of Jesus and the earliest Church in this matter and a flight from theological assessment of what status the alleged views of Jesus on such a matter might be deemed to have in the twentieth-century Church. There would appear to have been a flight also from the actual pain and social messiness of the present state of affairs under existing legislation—mitigated only by promises of increased support for the family etc. in the future. The Roman Catholic authorities appear to those outside (and to how many within?) to take refuge in processes of ecclesiastical annulment in order to save the letter at the expense of the spirit. One listened in vain, during the debate leading up to the divorce amendment, either from antagonists or proponents of the amendment, for any note of self-criticism. How could it be that the Church, which controls so much else, could have failed so signally to prepare people for marriage? What had our society failed to do in support of young inexperienced married people? What are the social and economic consequences for couples who take *Humanae Vitae* seriously? And, if they do not, is this a place where they may be said to incur 'guilt'? or not? or what?

It was edifying to read in Dr Daly's statement, quoted above, that one of the considerations to be borne in mind was 'the inconvenience which the present law and practice cause to people of other religious persuasions'.[7] This was a characteristically charitable recognition that one of the primary considerations for Christians in making up their minds is the hurt which failure to change may be causing others. It is very unfortunate if the edge was taken off that by the following consideration to be borne in mind, with which he concluded i.e. ' . . . a realistic assessment as to whether a change in the law would have any significant effect at the present time on attitudes towards the unification of Ireland'. This last clause in fact invites the conclusion that a change in the law would probably not change the attitudes of unionists. One must ask whether it would make it morally more proper—and that is what a bishop ought to be talking about—to pass divorce legislation if we thought that by doing so we would soften the unionists up a bit.

Weighing the consequences in the light of all considerations, including a number not usually taken into consideration, is certainly a very important part of the whole process of decision-making. If, for instance, one is proposing to alter legislation in order to lift a burden of oppression from some social group or other, it goes without saying that you must consider, from the experience and evidence available, what will be the probable consequences for them and others of the changes you propose to make. The bishops were asking us to do that. But too few of those involved took seriously during that debate, even though there were plenty of marriage and family law experts telling them, the degree of human suffering already involved which, however inadequately, the proposed constitutional legislation at least intended to address. Certainly those who opposed the change refused, by reference to the biblical witness, the long history of the Judaeo-Christian tradition and the insights gained from a sociological reflection on that tradition, to tease apart (1) the ideals which might properly inform Christian marriage, family and rearing, and (2) the actual social unit we have now or had till recently in Ireland which we have dignified with the term 'the Christian family' and spoken of as though it was an immutable social phenomenon. A serious pastorate knows that the pattern of family life we have had in the countryside cannot survive in the town; that longer life-expectancy, contraceptive practice, the liberation of women and many other things are changing the shape of our 'family' units even as we speak. Without turning our backs for a moment on fidelity, chastity, commitment, care of the vulnerable etc. we must recognise that these are only ever exercised *historically*. We must, when we turn to the biblical evidence, guard against turning Jesus into the legislator he consistently refused to be—not least with reference to this particular question.

The way the bishops handled the two referendum debates shows that they know where the appeal and the power of the Irish Catholic Church lies today. Decreasingly does it lie in any fear of excommunication or hell-fire or damnation, to be avoided by full participation in the sacramental life of the Church. Rather, as Tom Inglis has put it:

> Given that in most areas of Ireland the population is almost exclusively Catholic, the practices by which one comes to be regarded as the same as everyone else, the criteria by which one is judged civil and moral, are strongly influenced by the Church. To be accepted and regarded as a moral member of the community, one traditionally has had to engage in the rituals and socially approved practices of the Church, and not publicly contravene or criticise its teachings.[8]

In other words, the Church through its schools, social cultural and sporting clubs etc., has provided the norms in terms of which people understand themselves, however lightly they sit to it. As we have noted above, the Church has been a major source of political stability in modern Irish society. In the face of civil war, ambiguous attitudes to the new State and participation in its organs, the Church has been the real and durable *social* cement of society. At a time of such uncertainty as this, in the prevailing disappointment and disillusionment due to the 1960s the Vatican Council and the Lemass era not delivering everything which they seemed to promise, and in a society in which rich and poor are drifting further apart and the level of crime rising, it is not surprising that it was possible during the referendum debate to frighten people into taking no action on divorce legislation. Ordinary people do know perfectly well what is happening to marriages here and there all over the country. But, if the one body which seems to maintain equilibrium as everything else is shaken to its core, states that it is not happy about the introduction of divorce, and that body has fairly benevolent control over the earliest authority structures people encounter, most people will opt for no change. So it would appear that, at the level of tactics, and perhaps even of strategy, the bishops were right to concentrate on the probable consequences of change. They were not responsible for raising the spectre of the *expense* of introducing divorce, but of course that helped.

The victory at the polls may, however, turn out to be pyrrhic; for the bishops, in their anxiety to get the desired result there, in fact abandoned the high ground. For generations they were in a position not to have to answer for the stances they took: but television and the other media are hard to resist, and certainly since the time of the Forum, but arguably somewhat earlier, they have entered the world of PR. In the 'pro-life' referendum and subsequently in the divorce referendum, however, they chose by and large not to discuss the matter at issue or their own stance in either biblical or theological terms. Two hundred years of historical critical study of the New Testament need never have happened. Instead, they made the choice to confront an increasingly nervous and uncertain electorate with warnings about the possibly dangerous consequences of the proposed change. In doing so, they appeared to have a livelier sense of the dangers which may be attendant on the introduction of divorce legislation than they had of the empirically observable sufferings of men and women and children in a society in which divorce is not a possibility.

All in all, what we observed in those two referenda was a curtailed and stunted substitute for what was once called 'informing the conscience'. An outside observer might be pardoned for concluding that what the bishops were saying was: 'Of course, you are free to make up your own minds, and you must obey your conscience. But, if you don't do as I would like, you'll hurt mother terribly.' That line of persuasion is usually called emotional blackmail.

Reference was made at the beginning of the chapter to the distinction drawn by the bishops in 1986 between questions which are *moral* and those which are *political*. This distinction can often be perfectly clear. It is, for instance, hard to imagine that a decision on whether or not to decimalise the currency or to drive on the right side of the road could ever be regarded as, in any real sense, moral questions. On the other hand, a proposal to abolish capital punishment or re-introduce the birch must be so regarded. And no matter how difficult it may be to know how they are to be combated, hunger and poverty must also raise moral questions of great moment: and on these the Irish bishops have spoken well.

Somewhere between these 'political' and 'moral' questions there are others: for instance, proposals to nationalise or privatise a particular industry may be regarded by one side as 'merely political', while the other side may see it in distinctly moral terms. Christians and others, without for one moment denying the political character of specific issues, will often want to be the ones to insist on the moral dimension—often to the exasperation alike of conservatives and of Marxists. Presumably, the outrage which the present Bishop of Durham brought down on his head when he called Mrs Thatcher's administration a 'wicked government' was due to shock within the Conservative party to hear a bishop of the established Church associating 'wickedness' with a particular kind of economic and social policy.

When the Irish bishops in their pastoral letter *Marriage, the Family and Divorce* (1986) said that 'the questions raised in this debate are not simply political. They are also moral,' few would disagree with them. But what some of us may fear is that whereas those questions on which the Roman Catholic Church has specific regulations are unquestioningly to be regarded as 'moral' questions, other issues which are more open, and on which the Church has no specific line, apparently are not. If this is even partly true, surely it leaves the proportion of 'merely political' questions too high, and the proportion of 'political-and-moral' questions too low? Is there not a very extensive overlap?

The notion that only a small proportion of political questions are in fact also 'moral' ones lies uneasily side by side with the oft-expressed demand that Christians should be aiming to make as close a connection as possible between their religious practice and their daily lives. But it seems that the hierarchy is officially and expressly interested in that connection being made primarily with reference to only one part of the lives of the faithful. Being 'a good Catholic' seems increasingly to have to do with conformity to those regulations which differentiate Catholics from others. The Church runs the risk of turning itself into the more or less influential *religious* factor in the secular situation. Once such a role has been adopted, those in charge will readily come to believe that effectiveness is to be measured in terms of the extent of that influence and power. They will recall with satisfaction that in 1974 seven out of ten Catholics said that in a conflict between their occupational demands and their 'religious' obligations, they would obey the second. They will be hoping against hope that this proportion has not diminished in the intervening years. But perhaps what should cause them most disquiet in that statistic is the narrow meaning accorded to the word 'religious'.

9

Conscience as Consciousness of the Other

The informing and development of conscience is necessarily a *process*—whether one is speaking of the process whereby the believing community comes to organise itself and make rules for its own members, or the process whereby it confronts public issues and attempts to change the society in which it lives and in whose processes it is participant. As we suggested in the last chapter, the experience of the Roman Catholic Church over the past fifteen or twenty years in this regard is particularly significant, though in the end sadly disappointing. That experience would seem to suggest that, whatever about the past, in future

(1) the process of conscience-forming and decision-making must be rather less paternalistic than heretofore;
(2) there is going to have to be much more give and take between leadership and the faithful;
(3) there will have to develop a cheerful recognition of the probability that Christians, and even bishops, will inevitably disagree—even quite sharply disagree—on specific issues.

In the light of these and other probabilities, it is perhaps worth noting that the Greek word we translate as *conscience* carries within it the meaning *consciousness.*[1] Often it is better translated in that way. So it can mean, for a writer like Paul, consciousness of how things appear to God and therefore of how they really are.

Conscience in the Hebrew tradition may not be a unit of theological discourse, but it is nevertheless true to say that throughout that tradition it is in the encounter with the wholly other in other people, in God, that the transcendent reality is touched. Emmanuel Kant distinguished clearly between all other imperatives and the moral imperative of conscience. The moral imperative of conscience does not make its appeal to our desire for reward or appetite for high reputation among neighbours and friends. It does not rest upon our fear of hell-fire. Rather, it simply demands that I do *something* about, let us say, the old woman I see being mugged, even though it may be difficult to know exactly *what* to do, or about the child who has got into serious difficulties, swimming in the canal. It is because most of us assume the existence of this imperative that the young guards at Dachau and Buchenwald shock us so profoundly. Or when we heard of two young British soldiers who drove unwittingly into a funeral in Belfast being dragged from their car and beaten to death with no one to call 'Halt!', we felt that something had gone dead in the crowd. What had died was conscience. We sense that something has to have been anaesthetised if people are to go out in the middle of the day, throw a bomb and then return to play with their children and eat a good dinner.

A leader of Sinn Féin, speaking at a private meeting some years ago, explained how a lull in the bombing campaign had been due to a shortage of volunteers who had crossed what he called the 'sound barrier' which would enable them to do just that.[2] From Kant of course we learn that the moral imperative cannot be proved or demonstrated. Nevertheless, it remains something that most of us either respond to or deliberately ignore; it presents itself to us in terms of the call, the need, the demand of the irreducibly other.

The God whom the tradition of Israel speaks of and to is the one who 'intervenes' on behalf of the oppressed slaves. The presence of Yahweh makes itself felt to Moses at the bush as the uncontrollably other who recalls Moses to the plight of the others: 'I have heard the cries of my people under their taskmasters, and I have come down' (Exodus 3:7). Only later in their theological thinking did the Hebrews affirm that this God also *made* the world. The mythic stories of the Yahwist concerning the creation of Adam and Eve and their fall from innocence are primarily about the role of *homo sapiens* in a God-given world. The creative act of God is pre-supposed, of course, but it is the action of humankind which, for the most part, determines the fate of the world. So it is that when Adam and Eve sin, the ground is cursed '*because of them*' (Genesis 3:17). It is the actions and stances of humankind that bring about the horrors of childbirth, the brute suffering involved in agriculture, human labour and exploitation (Genesis 3:16–19). Indeed, the grotesque slavery of the female condition and the drudgery and exploitation of so many are the result of 'the fall', and reach their climax in the fratricide of which the story of Cain and Abel speaks in Genesis 4:1–16.[3]

After the disobedience of Adam and Eve, the Lord God, 'walking in the garden in the cool of the day', calls out to the man and the woman who are hiding from God's presence in the trees. God says, 'Adam, where art thou?' After Adam and Eve have shattered the relationship with God, significantly by doing what they should not to one of the trees of the garden, the altogether Other draws so close as to render their efforts to distance themselves impossible, even ridiculous. The sexual polarity which should be the source of open joy and complementarity is now to be disguised. The altogether Other, relationship with whom is seen as the chief end of Adam and Eve, confronts them with the persistently significant and unavoidable question. That where-question in effect insists that that relationship cannot be terminated by man and will not be by God—'Adam, where art thou?' In the Cain and Abel story, the same presence manifests itself with a question, at once similar and yet significantly different. In this case, immediately after Abel's murder, God says to Cain: 'Where is *your brother, Abel*?' The *other*, whom Cain had annihilated, still has to be accounted for. Whereas the man and the woman were called out of their ineffective hiding place into the inescapable primal presence Cain, in that presence, is faced with the question about his absent brother. Just as relationship with Yahweh defines the man and woman, so the relationship with his brother defines Cain. For he is his brother's keeper; that is precisely *who* he is. And Abel cannot be annihilated without there falling upon the head of Cain the excommunication, which is immediately pronounced upon him:

> God said, 'Now *you* are cursed (excommunicated) from the ground, which has opened its mouth to receive your brother's blood from your hand. When you till the ground, it shall no longer yield to you its strength; you shall be a fugitive and a wanderer on the earth' (Genesis 4: 11–12).

From being a tiller of the ground, he becomes a fugitive on the face of it, terrified lest someone should now take his life as he had taken Abel's. The Adam and Eve story in Genesis 3 defines humankind in terms of inextinguishable relationship with Yahweh. The Cain and Abel story in Genesis 4 defines Cain in terms of inextinguishable relationship with Abel, the brother who appears to be more well-pleasing to the Lord God than Cain himself. Cain loses everything as he strikes down the brother he believes is standing between him and the light, between him and the God he wishes to please.

To sum up, then, it would appear that *conscience* is at least in part the poignant awareness of the other as that which defines me. The Yahwist who wrote these chapters, is stating clearly that the Creator made us in such a way that we encounter the transcendent reality in and through the other(s), or not at all. If *we* do not hear God in the groans of the hungry and the pitiful cries of the oppressed for mercy, it is certain that God does, as their blood cries out from the very ground on which they were clubbed down or starved to death. Either way, in one way or other, the inescapably Other insists on encountering us.

Among many examples of failure to develop conscience, so that it becomes a poignant consciousness of the other(s) as that which defines me/us, we may select and mention four—two briefly, and two at greater length.

(1) Irish Protestantism post-1912

In our terms the inescapable Other encounters us in the religious or political community we do not belong to—also, of course, in those from whom we become estranged, even though nominally they belong to the same religious or political community as we do. We have already suggested that what happened to Irish Protestantism in the first decade of this century was that it lost its nerve. Unable to dominate in the whole of Ireland, it settled for dominance north of the border and hoped for minority privileges south of it. Looked at from another point of view, what happened was that it lost its sense of mission. Of course, the sects and specialist organs of some of the major Protestant Churches continued operations fundamentally on the model laid down by the proselytising missionary societies of the previous century, engaging unsuspecting frequenters of fairs in what were called 'spiritual conversations' and inducing people too polite to refuse, to buy copies of the Bible or the Mission's tracts. More sensitive and aware elements, in the Protestant Churches, simply could not think what to do.

It is true that the Church of Ireland and in particular the Methodists did run philanthropic agencies which catered for more than their own membership. But this had always to be done prudently, with due regard to the possibility that they would be seen as proselytisers. Neither in the North, where it was all-important to maintain the settlement of 1922, nor in the South where most energy had to be expended simply on insisting on 'Protestant rights', did it turn out to be the case that the *others* defined Protestant identity in any constructive sense. Of course it is true that, however much they have hated the term, southern Protestants have in affect often been little other than 'non-Catholics'. So it was that Protestantism, which should exist only to be a mosquito-movement for the benefit of the whole believing community, has too often relapsed into being a more or less exclusive religious association. Protestants in Ireland should be the Christians who exercise the freedom afforded to them by not having to operate within the constraints involved in the Roman obedience, in order to say and do things which may help all of us towards a wider and more urgent discipleship. This is not on the whole how it has worked out.

(2) Unionists and nationalists north of the border

In the North the socio-political groupings loosely called unionist and nationalist still find it difficult to understand themselves, much less define themselves, with reference to the others. *Identity* has been discussed a lot over the past twenty years, but it is seldom discussed in terms of 'the other community'. Valiant efforts have been made to overcome this—notably during the time of the power-sharing Executive in the North.[4] Clearly power-sharing between the 'two communities' was a step forward in a political region which had known fifty years of unbroken one-party government. It taught both the members of the Executive and the community at large that executive authority can be exercised within a single administration by people whose long-term goals differ significantly. But perhaps it contained within it the seeds of its own destruction; for after all its members held the positions they did by virtue of belonging to one or other of the 'two communities'. It had therefore the effect of institutionalising the very division one would wish to see melt away or be transcended. The question arises as to whether it ever can be transcended, purely within the confines of Northern Ireland, or whether the two groupings can only by some other means be brought to interpret themselves, not separately but only in terms of the others.

Church leaders, synods, assemblies etc. have with exceptions contributed little that is positive in this respect. The phrase 'our people', meaning our Presbyterian, Catholic or Church of Ireland people is on their lips more frequently than it should be.

(3) Protestants and Catholics and the schools in the Republic

It can honestly be claimed that in the twenty-six counties the confessional divide is no longer politically significant in terms of party allegiance. It is not reflected in the party political structures; there is no Catholic and there is no Protestant political party. And this is a very good thing. Certainly Garret FitzGerald seemed set fair to be the fair-haired boy of a majority of Protestants during his first administration, but then he lost his favoured position over the pro-life referendum. Even during the period of his popularity, numbers of Protestants remained loyal in their allegiance to other parties. It is also true to say that in selecting candidates the parties have had regard in constituencies like

Dún Laoire-Rathdown or East Donegal, to the fact that there is a relatively large minority of Protestant voters in those constituencies. But even in such constituencies, the subjects in relation to which a TD would require to think of the Protestant voters as a cohesive grouping are few in number—issues to do with schools and the provision of certain medical facilities, particularly in the realm of gynaecology etc. With reference to most of the matters that are put before the electorate or come up for consideration in the houses of the Oireachtas, Protestants do not arrive at their decisions or cast their vote as Protestants but as citizens. By and large this is a good thing. The fact is that the majority of Protestants in the twenty-six counties are middle class, and certainly the most influential Protestants are middle class. Inevitably this means that class interests figure as prominently in the casting of their votes as they do in the case of their Roman Catholic neighbours. Any confusion which arises does so from the fact that, particularly with reference to education, Protestants and Catholics are considered separately by the Departments of Finance and Education. This separate consideration arises historically on confessional grounds: it is given continuing force in the minds of Protestants by the regulations of the Roman Catholic Church governing the upbringing of the children of inter-Church marriages. However, in actual practice, Protestant schools which are in difficulties are willing to make up their numbers by admitting Roman Catholic children, and of these some may very well marry some of the young Protestants they have sat beside throughout their schooling. But then, of course, by definition these are 'nice' or sometimes non-practising Roman Catholics.

When the Protestant Secondary Education Committee (the body representative of the four Protestant Churches involved in secondary education, charged primarily with the allocation of the government grant for Protestant secondary education) turns its mind to consider educational questions outside of its primary remit, it thinks almost exclusively of how this or that matter will affect 'our schools'.[5] It rarely if ever considers these in any broader context. The fact that, by choice or of necessity, many Protestant children attend VEC or community schools is rarely adverted to, except to think of it as rather a pity. When, for instance, the question of the six-year cycle for secondary schools which had existed for a long time in most of the twenty-seven Protestant secondary schools arose, it came as a pleasant *surprise* to the members of the PSEC to discover that they had allies in the Catholic sector whose schools also had a six-year cycle. The Minister for Education eventually conceded that the six-year cycle should be retained by those who had it already and would, as resources became available, be extended to all. It may safely be assumed from their previous record however that the Protestants will not be among those pressing for that extension, not even for the sake of the 2000 Protestant children in five-year cycle schools. The positions habitually adopted by this committee illustrate very clearly the way in which 'we' can alter meaning, almost without our noticing it. 'We' can pass on to our children what 'we' received from 'our' forebears in a way that is deemed to be difficult or impossible in a school run by a religious order or in a community school. 'We' are given money to enable this to happen, and this money enables 'us' to heave those Protestants who are not middle class into secondary school and thence with luck into the middle class. Those who do not accept what is on offer through the grant scheme can therefore safely, though perhaps with a tinge of regret, be ignored.

What has happened? In fact, what has happened is that a group of Christians, some of whom really are concerned to maintain a particular type of Christian school and are doing so most creditably, are also in fact representing the interests of a small fee-paying section of the secondary school system and pressing its interests, largely without regard to the educational opportunities and conditions of the vast majority of children and teachers in the State. But a committee of Christians, representing branches of the Church of Jesus Christ as the PSEC does, cannot possibly rest content with such a role. The claims of all the other children of the State whom the men and women of 1916 bade us cherish equally, form the only acceptable context within which we do our duty by those for whom we may have inherited a peculiar responsibility. No Christians can in good conscience agree to educate their children at the expense of other people's. What has happened is that a sort of re-contextualising has taken place by stealth, and it has placed the Protestant educational establishment in the twenty-six counties in an invidious position. Marlborough Street may be satisfied with it; the establishment may be content with it insofar as they are school managers; but insofar as they ever feel they must respond to any kind of prophetic calling, they cannot possibly regard it as an appropriate resting-place. The context is *all* the children; minority rights can and sometimes do cut across citizens' rights to the detriment of the latter.

Protestants in the Republic are at present faced with a choice between *schools for Protestants* on the one hand and *Protestant schools*, on the other. But being faced with a choice and actually getting round to making the choice are two different things, and one suspects that it will not be made.

By *schools for Protestants* one means schools maintained or provided for a *religious minority* whose conscience cannot allow them to have their children educated in the same schools as the Roman Catholic majority of children. The grant made to the PSEC is certainly made assuming and respecting that conscientious scruple. But it is hard to avoid the suspicion that the cheque is in many cases eventually received by Boards of Governors of *Protestant schools*, i.e. schools run by Protestants, more committed to their own continued management of privileged middle class institutions than to the unbroken transmission and development of the insights of Luther and Calvin and the sixteenth-century Reformation.

But the Roman Catholic authorities, whether at the diocesan level or among the religious orders are entering upon a position not entirely dissimilar to that of the Protestants, which ought to embarrass and disturb them equally. To put the matter very simply, Catholic schools are there to produce *young Catholic people*, competent to act within and upon their society. But the statistics thrown up by recent surveys suggest that, whatever else they are managing to do, they are showing a declining success rate in producing young Catholics. No one from another denomination should take pleasure in this failure, but everyone should note it and ask what happens next. The missionary imperative alone would call urgently in question the resources of time and money that are already being spent and, failing a radical revision of policy, will continue to be spent operating the present Catholic secondary school system. But, in the context of the concerns in this chapter, there are other imperatives. They have to do with reconciliation and social justice, and therefore not by any means dissociated from mission itself, and they call the present situation in question. For the danger surely is that Catholic secondary schools which were established, sometimes in the teeth of Protestant or State intolerance and neglect in the first place, to fulfil the primary aim we have mentioned, will now be maintained with a different primary aim, i.e. that of providing a social élite and maintaining a power base for a declining Church.

The admirable record of the Jesuits, the Holy Ghost Fathers, the Dominicans, the Loreto Sisters and others on questions of poverty and deprivation need not lead us to forget that these orders in the last century set up schools which were modelled at least in part upon the English public school—even down to playing cricket and rugby in preference to Gaelic football or soccer. The provincials of these orders almost certainly find themselves today the embarrassed/proud inheritors of schools set up to enable the rising Catholic bourgeoisie of the nineteenth century to take their place under the British Empire and overcome the initial disadvantage of having been born Roman Catholic. These particular orders had made a decision more or less exclusively in favour of the particular class from which the leadership of tomorrow was expected to be formed. Small wonder that these schools have continued to produce the leadership in many areas of professional and political life in the twenty-six counties since 1922—one of them even claiming the honour of having educated the leader of the parliamentary Labour Party! It would be quite unfair to give the impression that this had not given rise to disquiet within the orders. There is good evidence that it has, and that their inherited responsibility for their schools is increasingly undertaken within the wider context of the education of the under-privileged.

The attitude of the hierarchy to Catholic involvement in the secondary school system, in the light of the developments in the vocational area and the expansion of the sixties and seventies has been evolving. But the preoccupation of the Church/Churches with representation on the management boards of new Community Schools and Colleges has been unseemly, not least because it has served to reduce the Church to the status of being no more than the 'religious' element in the overall situation, sometimes tiresome to the planners but recognised as potentially dangerous, even vicious if provoked. Of course, it would be culpable naïveté on the part of Church authorities to ignore the importance of factors to do with the acquisition and maintenance of influence and power in education as in any other field of communal activity. But, when that has been said, it should also be conceded that the reservation of mandatory seats for representatives of the bishop or other ecclesiastical authority may not be the most appropriate way of exercising influence at this stage in history—especially if you trust your laity who have in any case for the most part been educated in schools under Church management.[6]

Churches which have allowed themselves to become no more than the religious element in the educational situation, must in conscience recall that it is not *Church interests* but precisely *the interests of all the children of the State* which matter finally. Christian involvement in education can never be reduced merely to the promotion of Church influence, however benign that may be. Much more important than ensuring that there is a crucifix on the wall of the school assembly hall is to ensure that those who pass through the school discern the crucifixion at the heart of the society in which they are growing up. At its best, Christian involvement in education has been the believing community's response to the voice of the unheard as they cry out to be liberated from enslavement.[7] At its best, it has been the endeavour to enable children to come to a point at which they can work *within and upon* society with dignity and confidence. This cannot be done without putting into the hands of all the means by which they might begin to discover who it is has the power and the wealth, and by what means they acquired and now retain it.

Church schools which themselves have a stake in the maintenance of the present structures of power or distribution of wealth can hardly fulfil such a function, or maintain credibility as followers of one who was executed by those who had most of both. At the moment we run the risk of doing little more than peddling increasingly sophisticated courses on how to operate within what is no longer called the 'country' or even the 'world' but the 'economy' or the 'world market'. What the Churches in Ireland North and South must ask themselves very seriously is therefore:

(1) Are they in earnest about the democratisation of education and as urgently committed to equality of opportunity as they could be?
(2) Has their commitment to separate education, variously patterned in North and South, ended up by militating against serious campaigning for (1) above?
(3) Is there a way in which Christian involvement in education could be redirected toward the wider ends and aims of which we have been speaking?

Christian *conscience* in this field cannot be formed without sharpened *consciousness* of the needs of all our children—indeed, probably not without consciousness of the world's children who cry out for dignity and confidence. Nobody's children should be educated at the expense of someone else's: their needs, their hunger, the oppression under which they live, the lies by which their minds and ours are poisoned must be our primary concern as our schooling is planned, structured and carried out.

Specifically Christian education cannot claim that name unless it is what may be termed education into *solidarity* with the poor and the oppressed. In such an educational experience, teacher and pupil alike may come to meet the One who stands at the centre of the believers' experience. Speaking of 'the moral imperative in which God consists', José Miranda has something to say which should give Christians pause as they involve themselves in the educational process:

> In reality, all that is needed for this imperative to arise is a person who needs our solidarity and our help, the 'other' who is not I and cannot . . . have been implicit in what I already was nor, therefore, in what I already knew.[8]

The task of the only education worth getting involved in is to enable that 'other' to step out of the shadows of my mind where (s)he had been carefully stowed away, and be identified so as to begin the process of setting both of us free. He goes on:

> Only the summons of the poor person, the widow, the orphan, the alien, the crippled constitutes the true otherness. Only this summons, accepted and heeded makes us transcend the sameness and original solitude of the self; only in this summons do we find the transcendence in which God consists. Only this summons provides a reason for rebellion against the masters and the gods in charge of this world, those committed to what has been and what is.[9]

Christians are committed in education to the transcendence of the 'original solitude' of the self and of human groupings hiding among the trees of the Garden from the ultimate encounter. Neither chemistry nor geography, history, law nor languages can properly be studied for their own sake but only ever as ways into solidarity. The analogy is with the child's acquisition of language: what the growing child is doing is feeling his or her way into the community by means of that which makes and sustains community, i.e. language. And, in the Hebraeo-Christian understanding, language is that divine gift by which humankind transcends itself, creates its own environment and in remorse and self-congratulation relates to that Other we call God. Significantly, the result of trauma often is that the traumatised develop serious *speech* defects or even cease to speak at all.

The educational task is to build stations on the road to what might be termed 'recontextualising'. Welcome as the introduction of development studies into our curricula has been, the question is raised as to whether it should appear as a separate subject or should rather inform the entire curriculum of the school. As a discrete unit it runs the risk of becoming merely one aspect of the educational process, rather than be the conscientising end towards which the whole process is directed.

(4) The Irish Churches in relation to one another, as worshipping communities

But perhaps the most serious failure to recognise that Other in the others on the part of Irish Christians, comes about in the realm of their own interior life as worshipping communities. For it is precisely in that area of their activity, in which they overtly and explicitly claim to relate to the Other, that is, in prayer and praise, that the various ecclesial communities are still most effectively cut off from one another. Of course, it goes without saying that there must be some communal order and discipline with reference to the organising of the sacramental life of a particular community. Both Catholic and Reformed ecclesiologies recognise, however various the terminology with which they give expression to the recognition, that the ministers of the Word and Sacrament must be chosen by God and recognised by the believing and ordaining community which is itself in apostolic succession from the earliest community of believers. This recognition represents a reverent submission to the one whose Word they are to be ministers of. However, insofar as the discipline and regulation governing the ordination of ministers in our various communions reflects seriousness and due reverence for the Word of a God who is 'one Lord', it is difficult to see how mutual recognition of the various ministries of that Word which have grown up in our separated communions can be much further impeded or delayed.

Let us take another example. It is now accepted among a majority of the Christians of the world that baptism is baptism into the one Church of Jesus Christ.[10] Most Christians repudiate the notion of a purely invisible or spiritual Church; they hold the Church to be the visible, though by no means wholly perfect community of the justified and adopted children of God on their way through the often painful process of sanctification. The Church into which they were baptised is therefore a visible entity in their understanding. But this understanding is seriously called in question by the life and practice of the institutional Churches themselves, who have not hitherto been able to give concrete expression to the notion that there is one single Church of Jesus Christ.

When the apostle Paul reminded the Roman Christians that all of them had been baptised into the death of Christ, he went on to say that just as Christ was raised from the dead so they were now to be 'raised to newness of life'.[11] Irish Churches share with others in the world a measure of blame for the fact that they have spoken of mutual recognition of baptism, as though this recognition could be isolated from newness of life together. Whatever the good intentions of those who first mooted the idea of mutual recognition of baptism, the result in practice has not been a sharing in the death of the other and a new life understood only in terms of the other members of Christ's body. The mutual recognition of baptism has in popular understanding been reduced to the level of a relatively insignificant political concession—without serious implications.

A particularly reprehensible case study could be made, in this connection, out of current practice with regard to what are politely called 'inter-Church marriages'. Others more competent have and no doubt will document that situation in detail. Suffice to say here that what appears to be happening when two people of differing Christian traditions wish to marry is that representatives of the two communities are rushed to the scene, rather as if an unfortunate accident had taken place and, over a long or short period with the couple, negotiate the scene and the *dramatis personae* of the marriage ceremony. In fairness it must be said that this is, as often as not, done with considerable sensitivity. It should also be said that the promises given by the Church representatives to share in pastoral care of the couple and any children they may have, are well-meant. Of course, these promises share in the general contemporary confusion about what is meant by 'pastoral care'. But, more importantly, it often appears that the couple, if seriously committed, have thought more deeply about the implications of their marriage than have the 'pastors'.

What has actually happened? Surely this: that two young people have fallen in love and come to the point of wishing each one to understand themselves only with reference to the other. Their Christian commitment prompts them to seek what Christians call the grace of God in the face of so awesome a re-orientation of the self. In the face of that re-orientation, they are propelled towards that ultimate Other. It is at this point that they are brought face to face with the official representatives of two Christian communities who officially recognise that by baptism both the woman and the man are members of the one body of Christ. It may well be that at their baptism the priest or minister emphasised that baptism is initiation into the *one*, holy Catholic and apostolic Church. But it is probably only now, at their marriage, that these young people first ask for that noble assertion, that sacramentally-sealed affirmation, to be cashed. Young people, whose love is a kind of parable of the love Christ bears his Church,[12] are confronted by Churches which are themselves inhibited in responding to that love in concrete action. The couple, who now understand themselves each one in terms of the other, are scandalised by Churches who still understand themselves each one in terms primarily of itself. The Churches are consequently placed in a weak position. Just at the point when they should be there as a signal to the young couple that even marriage involves more than two people, and that there are still others beyond them again, and that yet Another is bending over all in judgment and in grace, the Churches are rendered tragically incredible by their own blundering disobedience.

In Ireland we have persistently allowed conflict, whether between Catholic and Protestant or unionist and nationalist, or the class conflict, to define our relationship to one another. But this is an elementary and tragic error: for the conflict is either of our own making, as in the case of class conflict, or foisted upon us and our forebears and exploited by ourselves, as in the case of the confessional political conflict. Only by some reductionism or other, can the 'others' be defined only in terms of the conflict.

This is one of the points of the story about the remarkable encounter between Jesus and the Samaritan woman in John 4:1–30. The woman comes to the well at Sychar as Jesus shelters there from the midday sun and he asks her for a drink of water. She expresses surprise that he as a Jew and a man should ask her as a Samaritan woman for anything. Later Jewish rulings declared that Samaritan women could never be certainly pronounced to be 'clean', so how could one accept a drink from one? Yet he has asked her for a drink, having himself no bucket and no cup. What defines their encounter is neither Jewish-Samaritan relations nor the impropriety of his being alone with a woman in what at midday would be a solitary place but rather *his thirst* and as it turns out, in a deeper sense, *hers*. The histories of their people do not define them; nor does theological controversy. That is the point developed in his response to her when she drags up the question of the rival claims of the shrines of Jerusalem and Mount Gerizim. Both shrines are relativised by what God now is seeking:

> 'Woman, believe me, the hour is coming when neither on this mountain nor in Jerusalem will you worship the Father . . . But the hour is coming and now is, when the true worshippers will worship the Father in spirit and in truth, for such the Father seeks.'

This passage explicitly acknowledges the value of the individual tradition, even while still in conflict with another, and it acknowledges the capacity of each tradition to nourish its adherents. To be 'even greater than our father Jacob who drank from this well and his sons and his cattle' is to be great indeed. But the woman acknowledges how wonderful it would be to have access to a water that could quench a thirst that even the water of her tradition could never permanently slake. She ends by begging for it from this apparently ill-equipped stranger.

It is not the battle-line of group conflict which defines, though it may blind or demean. What defines is the other's/others' need and what I/we are less prone immediately to acknowledge: that is, *my/our* need. And beyond that again is the acknowledgement that it is in receiving that we are judged and, in the full sense, saved. Jesus asked her for a drink, and she said:

> 'How is it that you, a Jew, ask a drink of me, a woman of Samaria?' Jesus answered her, 'If you knew the gift of God, and who it is that is saying

> to you "Give me a drink", you would ask him and he would give you living water.'

The woman is inhibited by tradition, history and proprieties from responding to the stranger's need. *A fortiori* she is blind to the possibility that she could possibly receive anything *from* him.

However much we may cherish our particular tradition—the European, the Catholic, the Protestant, or the Western tradition, the British, or the Gaelic tradition which have made us what we are—we are not ultimately defined by the terms of the conflicts into which Catholicism or the First World or Protestantism have been drawn. But we *are* defined by the others' needs and capacity to give—the rich nations of the world are defined by the debtor nations like Mexico and, in a small way, Ireland. Some economists are now pointing out that if the rich insist on demanding their pound of flesh, they will ruin themselves as well as the poor. So here at home the settled community is defined by the travellers, the free by the imprisoned offenders, the privileged by the underprivileged, men by women, heterosexuals by gay people, and on each side of the border the confessional majority by the minority.

Irish Christians, perhaps more than most, have to remind themselves that their worship is itself an exercise in re-contextualising, in conscientising. It has no meaning at all unless we recognise that the worshipping and believing community is itself defined by the world, God's love for which is explicitly what is being celebrated every time believers meet. 'This is the cup of the New Covenant in my blood' we repeat at every eucharist, 'which is shed for you and for all for the forgiving of sins' i.e. for the healing of that social dislocation which the woman at Sychar is caught up in, and which Paul calls 'sin'.

It is a measure of our capacity to head off what really would challenge us that, bitterly divided as we have been on the question of exactly how *Christ* is present in the eucharistic celebration, we have scarcely adverted in four centuries to the presence of the *world* at every eucharist. This is the point made so eloquently by the Catholic-Reformed group who, after years of meeting together at Les Dombes, finally produced a document which says among other things, the following:

> The eucharist is the great sacrifice of praise in which the Church speaks in the name of all creation. *For the world which God reconciled with himself in Christ is present at each eucharist: in the bread and the wine, in the persons of the faithful and in the prayers they offer for all mankind. Thus the eucharist opens up to the world the way to its transfiguration.*[13]

The central act of Christian worship does not take place in a quiet sanctuary apart from the world, any more than the incarnation does. When it is over, it is not the case that the worshippers are then sent back into the real world, fortified by the medicine of immortality. Quite the contrary. At the eucharistic celebration the world is altogether present and is arguably more 'real' there than at any other time. In that hour of worship it is, however fleetingly, presented as being without autonomy and as having no existence apart from the altogether Other upon whom it has presumed to pass judgment, but upon whose grace we hang dependent. Those who celebrate the eucharist acknowledge this: according to Paul they eat and drink damnation to themselves when they do not.

10

Conscience as Awareness of the Imminent and Creative Function of the Future

As we noted in the Introduction, the prophets of Israel, after all their efforts to give political expression to the dream of a people at one with Yahweh their God, seem to have concluded that that was not going to be possible—so, frustrated in their aim of establishing the kingship of Yahweh in Israel and Judah in the present, they began to think of God's kingship as belonging essentially to the future. This future they thought of as giving shape and meaning to their fragmented present. The coming kingdom is thought of as already in being in God; it is for men and women here and now to seek to discern its contours, and give it expression in terms of present realities.

It may be that today, immediately after the collapse of Stalinism and the demise of the Eastern socialist experiment, we are particularly reluctant to give too significant a role to the future or to the end or goal of history. We may feel that we have seen too many horrific sacrifices among those who were deemed by the party to be standing in the way of progress or impeding the course of history. The consumer society, now in the ascendant, appears not to need or to welcome the idea that there is an end towards which we move, since consumerism is an end in itself.

But when the excitement dies down, we may feel free to consider that, simply because horrible crimes have been committed and justified by the great end in view in the East, does not mean that Marx was entirely wrong in thinking that there is a goal or in insisting that the future should be the creative ingredient in our shaping of the present. Indeed, it has been argued that in this respect Marx was drawing consciously or unconsciously on the Jewish tradition.

Whether he was or not, that insistence is entirely consistent with one strand of meaning to be found in the word *conscience* which we have not so far adverted to, i.e. its orientation towards the barely-known future.

1. Conscience as consciousness of the creative future

The New Testament writers, in particular Paul, seem to think of Christian existence as being, as it were, suspended between the crucifixion of Jesus by the powers of this world, at one end, and the general resurrection of the dead, at the other. The raising of Jesus from the dead they understood as a kind of anticipation of that general resurrection at the end, when God will be all in all. As such, it is a challenge to faith, a challenge to set out on the way that led him to the fate he met. The God, into whose prevenient reality we are feeling our way is, according to the Christian understanding, none other than the God we have already met in Jesus Christ.

According to this line of thought, a new beginning for all is opened up in the resurrection of the crucified Jesus, a new way of relating to one another and to the creation. Conscience, then, can be thought of as that enlarged and imaginative consciousness which actually recognises a *new creation* in process, as wonderful as the first one (2 Cor. 4:6). In this process, not only are the apostles like Paul and his associates seen to be ministers of God's reconciling action, but as exemplary among the nobodies and nothings of this world who have been taken up by God and made into *somebody* (2 Cor.4:18). Christian *conscience* is therefore the dawning awareness of a new creation in process, with quite different presuppositions and starting-points from those assumed by the powers that put Jesus to death—a new creation which is drawing people forward into God's future. Cf. Romans 8: 22–25.

Of course, *conscience* can be used in such a way as to point up a more negative function. A glimpse of how things might be, or indeed already are in God, can serve to generate an acute awareness of incongruity, anomaly or guilt, a sense of just how I/we are out of tune with God's reality. In popular parlance, this is called 'having a conscience/a bad conscience about' something. It is just possible that some of the contemporary problems examined in chapters 8 and 9 have their point of departure in the recognition that this negative function has tended to be over-emphasised in the Western Church in general and in Ireland in particular.

In fact, however, the *conscience* of believers which has to be developed and informed is linked by early Christian thinkers to the obligation of Christians to bear witness to what *is* not yet, or more accurately, to what is not yet wholly visible. It belongs, therefore, more to the realm of faith than to the realm of knowledge or sight. We do not always respond adequately to its prompting, but neither does it always speak with absolute clarity. The New Testament writers never claim that their religion gives them infallible answers to all the imponderable mysteries posed by human existence—not to speak of pat answers to political questions! What they do claim is that believers have been granted the 'mind', the intentionality of Christ (1 Cor.2:16). They have been pointed in a certain direction—towards the mysterious agony and abandonment of the crucified Jesus. It is within shelter of the daring idea that the crucified one has a future which we can share, that the Christian conscience/consciousness germinates.

2. Kingdom and the future

Another term, used by Jesus himself in this case, which has this forward thrust or future orientation is that of the 'kingdom of God'. In the proclamation of Jesus himself and in the understanding of the gospel writers, the kingdom/kingship of God is pressing in upon our reality with liberating urgency and, at the same time, beckoning us into a barely imaginable future.

The judgmental aspect of this imminent kingship is not forgotten, of course. At the end of the parable of the unjust major-domo (Luke 16:1–8a), the Lord commends this rascal because he has acted 'prudently'. Presumably the sole commendable thing about him is simply that, in the light of a judgment already pronounced, he acts decisively, urgently and intelligently. Of course, what he actually does after dismissal is no less reprehensible than what he had done before he got the sack. But it is decisive and urgent, and it does perhaps dimly reflect the recognition that from now on, if he is to have any future at all, it is going to be one in which he is totally dependent on the good will of others—especially of those whom he had rather looked down on hitherto, that is, his employer's debtors.

The positive aspect of God's kingship is brought to expression again and again in what we have of Jesus' proclamation, for instance:

> The kingdom of heaven is like treasure hidden in a field, which a man found and covered up; then in his joy he goes and sells all that he has and buys that field. (Matthew 13:44)

The heart of this parable, as of the one which follows it, is the experience of the man whose spade unexpectedly hits against the lid of a box with coins in it, and his joy. This discovering and this delirious joy lead him to buy the field and to positive action for the future of himself and his family.

What the digger and the pearl connoisseur in the following parable represent is the joy of those who stumble, in their varied milieus, upon the totally unmerited dimension to human existence—which, of course, was there all the time without their realising it. When God comes close in rigorous demand and unconditional forgiveness, Jesus says that people tumble to the fact that the really valuable things like love, forgiveness, being taken seriously, trust, cannot be demanded or bought or fixed, but are only ever received or stumbled upon. The kingdom can only ever be received, as a child receives—totally without embarrassment (Mark 10:15).

It is widely agreed that the parables of Jesus are to be understood in the context of his action/his conduct. Whatever else is obscure about the outline of Jesus' life, one thing emerges with a degree of clarity from the records and that is, that his conduct both in Galilee and in Jerusalem was both anticipatory of the coming kingdom and, in a measure also, was aimed at making it present in a real and in a challenging way. His exorcisms and healings are understood by the primitive tradition in this way too. It also seems appropriate to interpret the meals, which he ate so often in the company of such varied people, as anticipations of the feast in the kingdom. Certainly, he often celebrated with people whose rough experience of life had predisposed them to tumble to this unmerited dimension in human existence. In other words, much of what he is recorded as saying is directed at a present which is being shaped by the future.

The tradition also records such a saying as Mark 8:38: 'Whoever is ashamed of me and my words in this adulterous and sinful generation, of him will the Son of man also be ashamed when he comes in the glory of his Father . . . ' which affirms the eventual and ultimate significance of what is happening in and around Jesus now in the present. This is also the case in one of his parables which tells about a farmer who is set free to do other things between sowing and reaping. But at the harvest, what has been going on first below the ground and then above the surface, will be shown up for what it is. This theme is given elaborated treatment by Matthew in the parable of the tares (Matthew 13:24–30), a parable of the kingdom which anticipates the basic orientation of resurrection faith itself.

For faith in the risen one is, as it were, faith in the goodness of the seed God has sown in Christ; it is courage to believe that the evil has no meaning except insofar as it is an attempt to subvert the good. And, most importantly for our reflections here, it is courage to receive the risen crucified one as the 'first fruits' of that general resurrection at the end. The 'Spirit' is that in God which challenges us to the risky possibility of such a faith, in mind and action. It is surely significant that Paul, for whom the resurrection of Jesus Christ is the first fruits, the challenging anticipation of that general resurrection which itself gives meaning and structure to our present life, scarcely uses the kingdom image at all. The kingdom has been replaced by the rhetoric of being in (i.e. belonging to) Christ, life in the Spirit, being conformed to his death and being raised with him. This encourages one to consider that these forward-looking eschatological images function for him in a way not at all dissimilar to the kingdom image in the synoptic gospels.

The well-known parable of the last judgment in Matthew 25:31–46 is not set in the everyday world of farmers, women baking, fishermen and merchants, as most of Jesus' parables are. The setting may perhaps be thought of as this world—in its ultimate and decisive hour. What is significant in terms of our preoccupations in this chapter is that neither those who are adjudged unrighteous nor those who are adjudged righteous are aware, even at this time, of the *ultimate* significance of what they have done or failed to do for others. They both ask equally, 'Lord, when did we see you hungry or thirsty or a stranger or naked or in prison?' It is not until what Paul would call 'that day', that all these people in need are shown up unequivocally as having the significance which, of course, they had had all along. What now emerges, however, is that in these needy people both righteous and unrighteous were *ignorantly* encountering the Other. The hearer/reader of the parable, however, is left in no such ignorance. S/he is left in no doubt as to the identity of all those sufferers (vv. 40, 45): 'Truly, I say to you, as you did it not to one of the least of these, you did it not to me.'

It would appear that three New Testament concepts—conscience, kingdom and resurrection—converge, at least in this respect, that they all give to Christian life and morality a forward pull into a substantially different and constantly changing future. So, however menacing the future may be and however disappointing the present, our task is not to re-create the past, to run back to fetch the age of gold, to consult the rule book, or with a bad conscience to stitch together some sort of future among the debris of present and past horrors. Christian involvement in revolutionary change is born out of the impulse to allow what *already is* and *will be* to enter the present. The ecumenical movement itself is essentially a question of allowing that already existing unbroken and undivided Church to come to expression here and now. It is not a question of building it.

3. The Church and the post/pre-figurative dialectic

Margaret Mead, in her book *Culture and Commitment* questions the assumption which she attributes to 'the adult generation' that there is still 'general agreement about the good, the true and the beautiful.'[1] 'Such beliefs', she says 'are of course wholly incompatible with a full appreciation of the findings of anthropology, which has documented the fact that innovations in technology and in the forms of institutions inevitably bring about alterations in cultural character. It is astonishing', she concludes, 'to see how readily a belief in change can be integrated with a belief in changelessness, even in a culture whose members have access to voluminous historical records . . . ' It is indeed astonishing, but it happens e.g. among Roman Catholic leaders who pass on the deposit of faith as though the ever-changing circumstances of nineteen centuries could leave the words of the original kerygma unchanged in meaning. And it happens among contemporary Irish Protestants like the Rev. Warren Porter who, while speaking at an Orange meeting in Rossnowlagh in 1986, reportedly committed himself to the following view of the Protestant Reformers:

> A Protestant was simply a sixteenth-century Christian living out first-century Christianity. A Protestant today should be a twentieth-century Christian who is living first-century Christianity.[2]

Interestingly enough, the newspaper account went on to report Mr Porter as saying that patriotism was 'being a good citizen wherever God in his providence has placed us'—which leaves patriotism with more flexibility than Christian obedience.

Margaret Mead's book traces the movement through what she calls *post-figurative* societies to *co-figurative* and finally to the *pre-figurative* societies to which, she claims, we all now belong almost without exception, in every part of the world. By *post-figurative* cultures, she means those 'in which children learn primarily from their forebears'; by *co-figurative* she means those 'in which both children and adults learn from their peers'; and by *pre-figurative* she means those 'in which adults learn also from their children.' Of the post-figurative she speaks as follows:

> Post-figurative cultures, in which the elders cannot conceive of change and so can only convey to their descendants this sense of unchanging continuity, have been . . . characteristic of human societies for millennia.[3]

Co-figuration Margaret Mead sees in terms of a transition from the post-figurative, in which the elders are the only source of authority, to the pre-figurative, in which adults learn from children. She notes that in co-figurative societies 'the prevailing model for members of the society is the behaviour of the contemporaries, but it is very rarely the only form of cultural transmission.'[4] She notes that often in the co-figurative society the young 'look not to their peers, but to their elders for the final approval of change' and indeed, 'each individual, as he successfully embodies a new style, becomes to some extent a model for others of his generation.'[5]

What Margaret Mead, writing in 1969 after more than forty years of anthropological research, fieldwork and teaching, was concerned to alert her readers to was what she deemed to be a wholly new cultural and sociological phenomenon. In studying and describing that phenomenon she suggested we might illuminatingly apply 'the pioneer model—the model of first-generation pioneer immigrants into an unexplored and uninhabited land'.[6] Pointing to the qualitatively different world which, in her view, is created by the communications revolution and medical technology, the emergence of a world community and the nuclear age, Margaret Mead sees children today as facing 'a future that is so deeply unknown that it cannot be handled, as we are currently attempting to do, as a generation change with co-figuration operating within a stable elder-controlled and parentally modelled culture'. Transferring the immigrant model from place to time, she puts it this way:

> Even very recently, the elders could say: 'You know, I have been young and you have never been old.' But today's young people can reply: 'You have never been young in the world I am young in, and you never can be.' This is the common experience of pioneers and their children.[7]

Margaret Mead's plea is for commitment across the generations in this disturbing and challenging new state of affairs. She does see some role for the 'adults', but it is a humble one. The older generation still have the power; they shape the education of the young. The suggestion is that, when the young say that the pioneers have built a house on plans they brought from the 'old country', the young have the right to complain that it does not keep out the draughts. Father should set out with them to identify ways to build that actually take this new climate into consideration. In Mead's view the scope of the adult role in education has shrunk immeasurably from the authoritarian days of post-figurative culture:

> We must create new models for adults who can teach their children not what to learn but how to learn, and not what they should be committed to, but the value of commitment.[8]

In the new situation, in Margaret Mead's view, the past is simply past and that is all. She takes it for granted that 'the idea of orderly, developmental change is lost for a generation of young who cannot take over the past from their elders, but can only repudiate what their elders are *doing now*.' She comes nearest to granting a positive role to the past, remote and recent, in the following:

> The past is the road by which we have arrived where we are. Older forms of culture have provided us with the knowledge, the techniques and the tools necessary for our contemporary civilisation. Coming by different roads out of the past, all the peoples of the earth are now arriving in the new world community. No road into the present need be repudiated and no former way of life forgotten. But all these different pasts, our own and all the others, must be treated as precursors.[9]

It is not necessary to enter into discussion with Margaret Mead about every detail of what she assumes or asserts here in order to applaud what is positive about it. Nevertheless:

(i) The general reader will note that although this book was written by a remarkably open-minded old person, it was nevertheless written by someone who had lived sensitively and perceptively through those heady days of the sixties when it was easier perhaps than it is now at the beginning of the nineties to believe that progressive forces were in the ascendant and would continue to be so. The 'children' of the 1960s in whom she placed such confidence and to whom she gave moving commitment have, many of them, in their thirties come to face in rather a different direction, often leaving it to those a decade or two older to hold aloft the flags they then waved so frenetically.

(ii) The general reader today will be conscious of the fact that Ms Mead was one of the most distinguished of a gifted generation of anthropologists, the whole thrust of whose work was directed towards drawing our attention away from the histories of the societies they studied and to concentrate rather on how they operated at the time when the anthropologist was studying them. Their fieldwork issued, not in histories of the Samoans or the Manus or the Nuer, but in descriptions of their life just then, at the time of the field investigation. It may be suspected then that Margaret Mead and those of her school have tended to underestimate the powerful continuing, creative and destructive role of the past in the present and in our plans for the future, in what we commemorate and in what we choose to forget.[10]

(iii) While welcoming the generosity of Margaret Mead's affirmation of the pasts of all those who, she says, are now arriving in the new world community, the Christian reader—but by no means only the Christian reader—may wish to gloss her expressed view that 'no road into the present need be repudiated and no former way of life forgotten.' If by repudiation we mean pretending such and such a thing has never happened, then of course, we would have to agree. If however we are being bidden in the name of academic detachment or in the interests of the future in a pre-figurative culture, to pass over the Third Reich or the purges of Stalin or the Ayatollah or the Boer Republic, then we must protest again that there are roads into the present or former ways of life which must be repudiated precisely in the interests of a healthy present and any future worth having.

Of course, Ms Mead was an investigator who no doubt felt that her scientific integrity could be safeguarded only by observing all ways of life with equal objectivity and awarding no points. To put it in terms she certainly would not have used, she wrote and taught as one who was professionally unconcerned with sin or with value-judgments. But, with reference to past, present and future, Christians are.

All this having been said, it is certainly worthwhile to take what is said in *Culture and Commitment* and, as it were, set it beside the New Testament. When we do so, certain interesting configurations of ideas emerge, particularly with reference to Margaret Mead's categories of culture: post-, co- and pre-figurative. There can be no doubt that religion, as the anthropologists have studied it all over the world, has been the instrument by which the elders have conveyed the proper way to conduct oneself in what is seen as essentially an unchanging world. Of course, a conquest or a natural catastrophe could alter this, but as often as not it did not, and indeed the community's sense of difference from their conquerors usually served to reinforce their own sense of peculiar and ineradicable identity. The history of the last 400 years has had this effect on Irish Catholicism, and Catholicism has been the primary distinguishing mark of the majority of Irish people, at home and abroad. The secularisation of many other parts of Europe and North America have up to now in Ireland had an effect similar to an invasion. Pope John Paul II on his pastoral visit to this country encouraged Irish Catholics to think of themselves as essentially a bulwark against invasive secularisation.[11]

Both Catholic and Protestant Ireland retained the essential features of the post-figurative culture until very recent times, and certainly the Churches are still organised largely on the assumption that we still live post-figuratively. Even when they are saying perfectly good things, the appeal of the magisterium of the Roman Catholic Church or of the Assembly, Conference or Synod is too often to the unchanging verities or to a primal golden age. The faithful faced with a bewildering world will, fitfully at any rate, be attracted by that, especially if and when their co-figurative behaviour patterns have come adrift a bit. This is presumably why parents so readily hand over the value-formation and religious education of their children to complete strangers, who have or who assume the role of elders. Among the young themselves, however, reaction to the education planned for them by a co-figurative society which nevertheless retains strong post-figurative features, will vary. The articulate are hampered in giving concrete expression to their demand for change by a lack of power. The inarticulate follow a passive role of non-cooperation, refusing to learn at school, or else co-operate in any casual work they may perhaps find, and are supremely uninterested in any conventional political activity. These exist in larger numbers than we usually acknowledge. But perhaps the largest and, in the end, the most destructive group are those who in an uninvolved and essentially exploitative way, comply with rules that are meaningless to them. But going through forms which no longer serve to educate those who accept them, can only teach students to regard all social systems in terms of exploitation, and a corrosive cynicism among the young is the unlovely result.

That this can happen in schools where there is greater or lesser Church influence is nothing short of a tragedy. But it does happen, because most of us who live in a co-figurative society for practical purposes, still hanker after a post-figurative one, and assume that at least the Churches are stable survivors from post-figurative times. Empirically studied, they almost certainly are for the most part. But the question arises: Should they be?

The pre-figurative culture which Margaret Mead thought she saw emerging everywhere may in fact be something of a chimera, but the Church of Jesus Christ could well be seen as being the prototypical pre-figurative community. Christianity was born into an eschatological, if not an apocalyptic cradle; the first Christians lived with the vivid possibility that annihilation was just round the corner and their earliest literature speaks of catastrophe, of a turn of the ages, the new day, new bottles for new wine, God's kingship bursting into our present and altering everything. It was the community of the new age.[12]

What marks Christianity out from the religions of the world is, at least in part, that it is *not* about how to behave in an *unchanging* world, but rather, if you like, about how to cope with a God on the move. From the beginning, and at the best moments ever since, it has seen change, not as a threat to the established order of things, but as the corollary of commitment to the God of Jesus Christ. In the Christian community, no special honour attaches to age as such. Honour attaches to those of any age who are born again into God's future and are allowing their presuppositions to be called in question—especially about 'what is good, beautiful and true.' It is not merely that in the believing community there is no longer male nor female, bond nor free; neither is there old or young. We learn most from those who have learned to receive like children and who, in varying ways, are living out of God's future, not their own past. Of course, there will be times when this is hard to do, when post-figuratively, the best we can do is look to see what others always did and do it ourselves, and other times when co-figuratively the best we can do is go along with what other believers are already doing, modestly esteeming others better than ourselves. But normatively, Christians are peering into that future into which in a measure they have already entered. Whatever course of action follows the sequence of liberation, expiation and reconciliation of which the cross is primal paradigm, is at least on the right lines.

The ethical life of the believing community is, as we have already said, suspended on a tense line between the cross and resurrection, of Jesus at one end and the general resurrection of which his resurrection is the first fruits, at the other. We are not encouraged, even by those gospel writers who gathered together as much as they could of what he had said, to turn him into what Martin Luther called *Mosissimus Mo*ses, the greatest law-giver of all, a provider of blueprints for our action today. What the New Testament does encourage us to do is to press forward towards God's kingdom. But an attentive reader of its twenty-seven books will recognise that in the Jesus story we are given certain criteria by which to test the spirits of the future to discern what is 'of God' and what is not. His constant widening of the context, his going back beyond Moses to the creation itself when he was asked about e.g. divorce, his going beyond the regulations concerning the shewbread to the urgency of the mission and the need of the hungry, his breaking through the purity laws in compassion, the whole way that led him to execution at the hands of those who represented the Pax Romana and those who sat in the chairs of Moses and of Aaron—all these give us, not detailed *directives* but a clear *direction.*[13] The work of the Holy Spirit is to dare us to receive the crucified one as risen and to aid us in discerning, not what Jesus would have done but what might be the mind of Christ (1 Cor.2:16).

Clearly choices are going to face us as a result of the revolution in communication, or the availability of nuclear power or our capacity to control conception and free women from being only baby-bearers etc. which are going to be very difficult indeed. But they are not just unfortunate accidents; they arise from God's future casting a sometimes almost unbearable light into our present, and the Churches really must come to look at them in such a way if they are to keep faith with God or humankind. The Churches in Ireland run the risk of holding on to the few and losing the many—not because they have courageously witnessed for Christ, but because they have either met new challenges with reference to allegedly eternal and unchanging verities or have trivialised serious questions by merely pragmatic manoeuvring. Writing of the Church in Paul's conception, J.C. Beker uses words that equally apply today wherever the believing community, both leaders and members, respond to their calling:

> The Church is not an aggregate of justified sinners or a sacramental institute or a means for private self-sanctification, but the avant-garde of the new creation in a hostile world, creating beach-heads in this world of God's dawning new world, and yearning for the day of God's visible lordship over his creation, the general resurrection of the dead.[14]

11

Recovering a Past which the Future can Use

We have already drawn sustenance from Paul Lehmann's phrase about 'the future shaping the present out of the past'.[1] With that phrase in mind, we have looked at the way it has been possible for the two 'major traditions' in Ireland to celebrate and bring to political realisation in the present their contradictory pasts, without much regard for one another and without either of them having a credible future in view. In chapter 10, we at last began to explore the sense in which the Christian vision, whatever about that of the Irish Churches, draws its inspiration from the coming kingdom and is summoned to a growing and ever more inclusive consciousness of others.

The question now arises as to how exactly the past is to be recovered from the stories we have used and misused, and may even come to function in that re-shaping of the present which the future is engaged in.

1. Jesus' past as raw material for the re-shaping of our present

In the last chapter we considered the way in which the Christian past, especially and normatively the events of the life and death of Jesus, monitors our reception of what the future seems to be offering. According to the Christian understanding, it is the Holy Spirit who dares us and enables us to receive the crucified man as risen and exalted, but also brings within our reach the 'fruit' of the Spirit in 'love, joy, peace, patience, kindness' etc. (Galatians 5:22–23). This chapter of early Christian history turns out to have more relevance to our situation that might at first appear—as we shall see.

The communities of Corinth and Galatia were exercising new capacities which they believed to be gifts of the Lord, transporting them into the world of the Spirit. But in fact the very exercise of these charismatic gifts was leading to the presumptuous dominance of one charismatic group over another, to spiritual pride and to serious divisions (1 Cor.1:10–11). Without denying that the gifts on which they prided themselves were in fact gifts of God, Paul says two things:

(1) he points out that they are gifts of sheer unmerited grace, and therefore there could be no grounds at all for pride of any kind, and
(2) in the reception of these gifts of the exalted Lord to the Church, he points the Corinthians, not *forward* to the realm of religious wish-fulfilment in trance and glossolalia, but, in fact, *backward* to the cross of Jesus and the way that led him to it. So he is able to say, with what is under the circumstances a pardonable one-sidedness, that he is determined to know nothing among them except the crucified Jesus. Paul insists that order, wholesomeness and direction can be restored to the believing community in Corinth only if they allow the story of the one crucified, by those with a monopoly on power and wisdom, to monitor and redirect the vision of the future they believe themselves to be invited towards by the exalted Lord.

2. Our own pasts as raw material for the future

The question still arises as to how we remember the past rather than merely repudiate it. The past is very often the story of how we have misappropriated and misused the gifts and vision God has given us in and through every culture and political system in world history. Our duty might be described as being to recover for ourselves and our children the gift more or less as it was before we misused it.

Christians are committed to the view that God's gifts do not return to God void, but accomplish the thing whereto God sent them (Isaiah 55:11). But the irrevocability of God's gifts has been alternately a problem and an opportunity in Christian theology and practice since the earliest days of the Hellenistic mission. In the light of the universal call to all—women and men, Gentile and Jew—in and through the crucified Messiah, the question arose as to the status now of Israel's past, its special call, the covenants and the Law of God, obedience to which had marked Israel out as God's special instrument and defined Jewish identity. That is the question to which Paul, the Jewish missioner to the Gentiles, was recalled again and again.[2] Whatever else may be said about his responses to that question, he does not appear to have been one of those who urged Jewish people to repudiate their Jewishness or turn their backs on 2000 years of Yahweh's dealings with them.[3]

It should go without saying that repudiation of a specific culture is a poor response to the realisation that Christianity must never allow itself to be linked exclusively to any one cultural/linguistic expression. For the fact is, that it is only in and through a specific culture that the faith can ever be transmitted and lived at all. This is not just an unfortunate accident. A particular language and culture is not the disposable wrapper in which culture or religion are parceled; it is their symbolic medium, infinitely precious and each time unique. Imperial powers recognise this in a grudging way every time they try to replace the native language of a subject people by their own.

If human culture is seen as the response of a given people to the initiatives and gracious gifts of the hidden Mover behind human history, then in spite of all the misuse of gifts there may be expected always to be something worthwhile to be recovered from their experience and their history—if only because of the one with whom it is an encounter. Among young people brought up in Ireland North and South over the past twenty years, it is possible to detect an impatience with the conflicts they have inherited which is wholly understandable. Their education and their experience of the world outside encourage them to reject what they identify as the provincialism of their elders and of those of their peers who are caught up in the conflict. They yearn either to get out altogether or to re-contextualise—to set the whole conflict in a wider context in which it may lose significance or even disappear altogether. Again, this is wholly understandable, and the quest for a new context is what the greater part of this book has been about.

But it is possible to settle for a false, or at least a dangerously inadequate re-contextualisation, one which might not in fact serve as a key to unlock and recover the past and open the future. Here we might mention two examples—one from the North, and one which refers more particularly to the South.

(i) The integrationist approach in the North

Integrationists take the logic of a United Kingdom as far as it can go.[4] They contend that Belfast is as much a part of the UK as Finchley. They by and large repudiate the goal of devolution for the North and propose that, perhaps with increased representation at Westminster, the people of Northern Ireland should be given the opportunity to vote for candidates put up by the British political parties, just like the English, Scots and Welsh. Those who put this idea forward express the hope that political life would be 'normalised' in Northern Ireland as a result and that the politics which turned every election for Stormont into a referendum on the border would be transcended by being brought more intimately into dialogue with those issues which preoccupy the Conservative, Labour and other political parties in Britain.

Many of those who propose integration really are concerned to enlarge horizons and deepen concerns by widening the context. But, aside altogether from the fact that they are ignoring the deeply ingrained feeling of the majority of British people that the Northern Irish are quite simply not the same as the people of Finchley or Yorkshire or even Scotland, the proposal is perhaps less liberal than may at first appear. Firstly, it runs roughshod over the aspirations of those who hope for and wish to be allowed to work for a reunited Ireland by forcing their party/parties into conflict with large British parties with infinitely greater resources. It may not intend to, but it does in effect rule out serious debate about reunification. Secondly, it enlarges horizons only in an eastward direction: it ignores the fact that, however different Ulster Protestants may feel from everyone else in Ireland, it is in Ireland they are living. Thirdly, it fails to address the possibility of Irish people understanding themselves increasingly as living and working together in a post-1992 Europe, in the only part of the EC not joined to the other members by road. Re-contextualisation, to be credible and to be magnanimous, must be as wide and dynamic as possible.

(ii) The European dimension

Having mentioned the European dimension in favourable context, we might just now say something less wholeheartedly positive about it. Those who feel stifled or cramped in Irish society are quite understandably aware of a certain liberation and release as they stretch their limbs in this wider context. This is certainly healthy, but again it can lead to an inadequate re-contextualisation. Through our membership of the Community, there is no doubt we are brought into contact with parts of the world and areas of conflict which we in Ireland have hitherto scarcely been aware of—and again, in a shrinking world, that is a good thing. But demands for the harmonisation of European Community foreign policy must not blind us to our origins or make us forget where we came from. Most Irish people's origins are not posed in wealth, no matter how far they may have travelled in a generation or two. Furthermore Ireland, as an EC member with a colonial past and arguably an unresolved neo-colonial present, has certain essential characteristics which give us as much in common with the Third World as with the First.[5] Instead of meekly following the lead of the rather confused former imperial powers as they seek a new post-imperial role in their policies towards e.g. South Africa or the emergent countries of Asia and Africa or the Arab States, Ireland should without question be on the side of the exploited and be responding unilaterally as best we can to the agonised calls for help they are sending out to us. Instead of rebuking ourselves for not 'playing our part' in what is euphemistically called 'Western security' shoulder to shoulder with the great arms manufacturers to left and right of us, we should be a voice for a system of international security, as, at our best, in the past, we have been. We should use our membership of the United Nations more actively to support those who are determined that it remains the instrument of international security it was intended to be, rather than a body which can be manipulated in such a way as to sanction the economic and military policies of 'great powers'.

In other words our commitment to a future inside a European community of nations must be monitored and given constructive direction by our own past experience if we are to emerge from the fire refined, rather than coarsened. If this happens, then our European vision, as the poor of Europe, could become a part of the infinitely wider search for a world in which peoples interdepend with dignity. The future would shape the present—not just out of the imperial pasts of France and Germany and Britain—but out of the colonial past of Ireland, the poverty and the exploitation. This will make for the widest possible re-contextualisation for everybody, and the most compassionate involvement with the poor and the hungry of the Third World whom so many in the First World are only looking for the opportunity to exploit all over again.

We have already considered the way in which the admirable principles of civil and religious liberty of the revolution of 1688 were subverted in Ireland, due to the fact that those who espoused them did not intend that that they should be applied to all. But when that has been said, as it must be, the principles are still good ones. Protestants of both the Episcopalian and Presbyterian traditions in Ireland could argue that any notions which their forebears ever developed of social justice and representative democracy, were in fact developed under the Protestant succession in a constitutional monarchy. That would be historically arguable and defensible. What is by no means defensible is the suggestion that today it is necessary to live under monarchy of any kind in order to cultivate or extend these rights. Furthermore, any unclouded vision of what has happened in Northern Ireland since 1921 shows up the fact that loyalty to the crown has been little more than a code word for Protestant domination. Precisely in order to release the liberties they say they prize, Protestant unionists should now seriously consider breaking the link with a loyalty which has only served to distort the original vision of the seventeenth-century libertarians. To fail to do so prompts the suspicion that they hanker after domination more tenaciously than they love those principles. Obsession with the doings of members of the house of Windsor is largely a middle class phenomenon and is in any case shared by people in a number of countries owing it no allegiance. It is an entertainment, on a level with 'Dynasty' and 'Dallas', and scarcely something that should be allowed to stand as an obstacle on the road to peace in Ireland. On the whole the obsession with royalty is not shared so enthusiastically by the working class Protestant, who prefers real soap opera with professional actors.

Again, it may well be argued that Protestantism has within it the potential for building up a sense of personal responsibility, and that it has a potential for developing representative democratic institutions. But, in the peculiar conditions of the North of Ireland it seems as if this potential is unlikely ever to be realised, as the painful inability to re-establish devolved local government clearly shows. The time may well have come to think of operating in a context other than the United Kingdom. That context clearly has been shown, after seventy years, not to be providing an environment friendly to democratic development. Unionists must recognise that the great principles of civil and religious liberty and the civil rights which any bill of rights we might draw up today would have to contain, are not safeguarded by the British crown any more readily than by many other forms of government or policies. With appropriate safeguards, in a new Ireland, Protestants would be liberated from the effort of trying to dominate, and the Ulster Protestant could once again with a clear conscience join battle in defence of the values Protestantism claims to stand for. Northern trade unionists would be released to stand shoulder to shoulder with those of the rest of Ireland, and it would be possible for Ireland to participate meaningfully in the peace movement and the anti-nuclear movement.

If we concede that what happened in 1912 was that Irish Protestantism lost its nerve, and that Protestant-unionists, discovering that they could no longer dominate in the whole country, determined that they would dominate in one corner of it, then it would appear to follow that the recovery of nerve and even of self-respect is dependent on Ulster Protestants once and for all abandoning the role of garrison for British interests and simply being themselves. As things are at the moment, especially since the signing of the Hillsborough Agreement,[6] it often looks as if the British recognise that their interests are as well served by Dublin as by the unionists of Belfast. Be that as it may, the practice of treating everybody else as an equal is inevitably going to take away the *raison d'être* of Northern Ireland. But it is going to have one great compensation: it is also going to set the unionist people free to contribute fully to the whole community in this island where they have lived very much longer than the families of most citizens of the United States have in North America. And once that happens, they will be more at home in the world outside as well.

In each case, something of the past which was comfortable must be sacrificed, but it is not to be compared with what could be gained. A past with which the future might shape our present would be to hand.

3. The revolutionary Enlightenment in the North-East as one possible key to the retrieval of the past

Let us now turn to consider *how* it might be possible to retrieve what was of value in the two traditions we have been considering, which was seriously distorted or even lost in the quest for dominance. We have already suggested that the Jesus story can serve as a monitor and guide in this enterprise—at any rate, for believers. But is there anything in Irish history itself which, if it were examined and set to work would have this liberating effect? Is there anything which could act as a key to unlock a past which has become distorted or has been even prostituted in the interests of pretentious claims made either by Protestant-unionism or Catholic-nationalism? Specifically, what we are looking for is a movement or movements of thought in which people have paused for a little while to endow received opinions or traditional story with a new meaning or an altered significance.

In many countries of northern and central Europe this happened in the sixteenth century, during the Protestant Reformation. In the course of that time, the story of the early Church and even the story of Jesus himself were re-examined both by reformers and counter-reformers, and as a result the whole social fabric underwent radical change. It is a matter of fact that Ireland had no native Reformation at this time to speak of. The rival confessions which have been locked in conflict since the seventeenth century in Ireland were formed later, by Calvinist orthodoxy on the one hand and the Tridentine theology of counter-Reformation on the other. The conflict was not the result of a debate which had originated on Irish soil, as it was in France or Germany. It was imported late in the day after attitudes had hardened and, almost from the start, was interwoven with the claims of the English crown to suzerainty over Ireland.

The second such *paradigm-shift* was the Enlightenment. Of course, it would be true to say that even in countries much more significantly affected by the Enlightenment than Ireland was, it was only a minority élite who were in a position educationally to take in what was happening.[7] In Ireland the minority was smaller still. Within the eighteenth-century Anglo-Irish establishment, this meant in effect the Fellows of Trinity College, some intellectuals among the Church of Ireland clergy and some individuals from the ranks of the professional classes who formed the membership of the Royal Irish Academy.[8] Some of these, like Edmund Burke, left the country altogether.[9] But those who stayed had privileges to defend and had no pressing reason to look for radical change, economic, social or political.

No such inhibitions affected that other significant body of Irish Protestants—the Presbyterian dissenters of the North-East, who smarted under political and religious disabilities only slightly less severe than those affecting Roman Catholics. It is of course true that, even as late as the mid-eighteenth century, it was not at first Roman Catholics or Presbyterians who promoted ideas of reform. Just as in France, the initial impulses to revolution came from the ruling class itself who had come to feel, like the American colonists, that their trade was suffering as a result of the subordination of their parliament to that of England.

The Volunteers, formed at first as a kind of local defence force against the contingency of a French invasion, became a force for threatening the government into improving the position of the Protestant colony in Ireland.[10] The story of gradual reform and the failure of radical reform in the Irish parliament of 1784 is too well-known to be repeated here. Suffice to say, what was achieved was quite insufficient to satisfy the radical element of the population which included many Presbyterians, as readily as it had satisfied the landed gentry of the parliament on College Green.

Evidence of how far thinking in Ulster among the Dissenters had progressed by May 1784 is provided by the 1st Volunteer Company of Belfast who invited 'persons of every religious persuasion' to join them. By the end of that same month, the 1st Volunteer Company was parading at the opening of St Mary's, the first Roman Catholic church to be built in Belfast, and a Presbyterian minister spoke from the altar steps. Ulster Presbyterians were fired by the news they were receiving from the former American colonies, where many of them had relatives. Copies of Tom Paine's *Common Sense* passed from hand to hand among the literate, and by the late 1790s his *Rights of Man* came to be known as 'the Koran of Belfast.'[11]

These Presbyterian people had been reared in a radical tradition which was normally conservative but which in Scotland had insisted that kings rule, not by divine right, but by covenant with their people. Under pressure from discrimination at home, side by side with the encouraging example of the young United States and of France abroad they were prompted to allow their radicalism to develop in a progressive, even revolutionary direction.

This can readily be seen in the life and thought of, for instance, Henry Joy McCracken and his sister, Mary Ann, born into the new Dissenter merchant class,[12] and of Jemmy Hope the weaver of Templepatrick, representing persons of no property worth talking about.[13] After the victory of the American colonists and movement towards reform in France it is reported that a picture of Benjamin Franklin was hung in a public house in Belfast, together with those of Mirabeau and Dumouriez. When the revolution in France broke out, it seemed to be the realisation of the hopes of reformers as well as revolutionaries in Belfast. The Northern Whig Club, complete with green cockades, met on the first anniversary of the storming of the Bastille, and among twenty-seven toasts proposed and drunk, were those of Mr Paine, John Locke, Dr Franklin and M. Mirabeau. In resolving to hold that celebration however, they had spoken of the revolution as leading the way to 'an orderly and gradual reform'.

By the mid-1790s, some had drawn back from the revolution, had given up the French lessons so popular in the Belfast of the early 1790s and left the field to those who were not so easily put off by the post-revolutionary bloodshed in Paris. On the way to the Battle of Antrim in 1798, Jemmy Hope's *Spartan Band* sang the Marseillaise. How important Mary Ann McCracken, for instance, felt it to keep in touch with thinking abroad and to keep reading is evident in a letter she wrote to her brother while he was incarcerated in Kilmainham. In it she recommends Godwin's latest book, at the same time judiciously criticising his work on *Political Economy*.[14] In another letter to him she encloses Mrs Wollstonecraft's book on the rights of women, commending it as 'a more pleasing amusement than drinking!'

This confluence of influences brought home to the United Irishmen and women a recognition of the catastrophic nature of sectarianism, as a force which holds back political and social progress. Mary Ann McCracken's letters are a consistent testimony to that. So is much else in the literature, including the sermon by Dr Steele Dickson at the Volunteer Church in Dungannon where he warned against division, probably particularly with division over the advisability of Catholic emancipation in mind, under the text, 'See that ye fall not out by the way.'[15] But it is to Jemmy Hope, the weaver of Templepatrick, that we turn for what may well be the most penetrating analysis of what was wrong. Writing of the 1790s many years later, he said:

> None of our leaders seemed to me perfectly acquainted with the main cause of social derangement, if I except Neilson, McCracken, Russell and Emmet. It was my settled opinion that the condition of the labouring class was the fundamental question at issue between the rulers and the people.[16]

There can be little doubt that it was under the influence of Hope that Henry Joy McCracken, by nature an egalitarian, began the difficult job of working in conjunction with a young Catholic United Irishman in Co. Armagh among the Defenders, trying to educate them out of their religious isolation and into joining the United Irish Societies. Speaking of his own early years and his first employer, Hope had this to say:

> The first three years I earned my bread with William Bell of Templepatrick, who took every opportunity of improving my mind, that my years would admit . . . he made me get forward my work and sit with him while he read in the histories of Greece and Rome and also Ireland, Scotland and England. Besides, his reading and comments on the news of the day turned my attention easily to the nature of the relations between the different classes of society.[17]

Nor did Hope see any fundamental difference between the plight of the rural labourer and the urban worker. In the country 'landlord' and 'churchlord', in the town 'manufacturer and commerce, fictitious capital, fictitious credit, fictitious titles to consideration, presented the numberless interests of the few, in opposition to the one interest of the many. Such were the difficulties with which the men of Ulster had to contend, besides that perplexity arising from a pensioned clergy, puzzling its followers with speculations above human comprehension, and instigating them to hate each other for conscience sake, under the mark of religion.'[18]

Sectarianism is not considered on its own, but is placed firmly in its economic context by this man of only fifteen days of formal schooling! There is a sad epilogue to these perceptions of his in a sentence at the end of one of Henry Joy McCracken's last letters, written to Mary Ann after the failure of the 1798 Rising. He was on the run, and he tells his sister in this letter of rumours he is hearing of friends betraying friends:

> You will no doubt have a great number of stories respecting the situation of this country; its present unfortunate state is entirely owing to treachery.

On the truth of the rumours reaching him he can make no detailed comment, but with melancholy realism, he concludes his reflections on the rising thus: 'The rich always betray the poor.'[19]

These radicals again and again show a capacity to look at the world outside without merely extrapolating from their own situation. Take for example the following recollection of Thomas Russell, who was one of them, given by Mary Ann McCracken in 1859, long after the period she is recalling:

> Thomas Russell in the days of Wilberforce abstained from the use of slave labour produce until slavery in the West Indies was abolished, and at the dinner parties to which he was so often invited and when confectionery was so much used, he would not taste anything with sugar in it . . . .[20]

At eighty-nine, with perhaps an inadequate grasp of the economic factors which were forcing emigration, she stood alone at the bottom of the gangway up to the American boat, distributing anti-slavery pamphlets, and urging the emigrants not to go. Nor were the rights of women forgotten in the Belfast of that time. Writing to her brother Harry in Kilmainham, Mary Ann laughs at the idea that because women's bodies are sometimes smaller than those of men, their minds also are. She draws attention to the diminutive stature of Mr Neilson and Atty Bunting, the editor of the first major collection of harp music, in spite of their considerable genius as people. She herself had been independently in business with her sister in the muslin trade since 1790, and kept that up for thirty years. She knew what she was talking about when with reference to women's education she said: 'Business they might likewise pursue, if they were educated in a more orderly manner.'[21]

Among Calvinists in general, a firm belief in a predestinating God who, by his 'eternal decrees had for his own good pleasure, foreordained whatsoever comes to pass',[22] could and often did lead to a kind of fatalism and a political attitude which was supine. From time to time, however, it has given grit to those who, like these United Irishmen and women, could not conceive of the divine will as satisfied with things as they are. This conviction gave them fortitude in the face of failure, knowing that present reverses are temporary and of passing significance only. In contrast with many of both right and left in the twentieth century, they had a strong belief that political life has moral dimensions. The following statement by Mary Ann McCracken may be faulted as being theologically inadequate, but nevertheless it has a certain fundamental strength:

> Some object to joining religion and politics together; but surely religion should be the ruling principle of every action and of every thought. With such an unerring guide, how could we go wrong?[23]

A robust commitment to the Calvinist doctrine of the sovereignty of God underlies all Jemmy Hope's writings on the land question, as in the following:

> The Most High is the Lord of the soil; the cultivator is his tenant. The recognition of all other titles, to the exclusion of this first title has been the cause of an amount of human misery, beyond all calculation . . . . [24]

It is considerations of that sort which provide the ideological base for his extensive writing on land holding:

> The soil is not like the objects of barter; it is the social capital from the cultivation of which all earthly wants are supplied . . . My concurrence shall not be given to the scheme of a delusive fixity of tenure, to enable the landlord to continue to draw the last potato out of the warm ashes of the poor man's fire and leave his children to beg a cold one from those who can ill afford to give it . . . A fixity of tenure? a fixity for ever in famine![25]

The story of how this minority of Dissenters 'defected' from the progressive cause has now been fairly well traced. Already in 1792, the government bought the acquiescence of the Synod of Ulster (Presbyterian) by increasing the Regium Donum.[26] But there were other factors: disillusionment with France; horror at the sectarian violence into which 1798 deteriorated all too often in other parts of the country; the emergence of the Orange Order; repeal being sought by the same leader who had gained Catholic emancipation; later in the century, the introduction of ultramontanist ideas with Paul Cullen; the industrialisation of Belfast which crowded it with Protestant and Catholic workers deeply affected by the sectarianism of the land-hungry in the countryside and which turned it into the very cockpit of sectarianism; the pan-Protestantism of Cooke and the evangelical movement, with its exclusive emphasis on personal salvation; the power exercised by the Churches as interest groups in what after 1870 had become a situation of denominational pluralism of sorts—these factors and others contributed to the eclipse of the progressive radicalism we have been glancing at. But, while it lasted, it was a wholesome and even at its best a noble thing.[27]

Their Calvinist emphasis upon the sovereignty of God in the creation and even their doctrine of predestination gave them a certain self-confidence in dealing with the powers that be which their economic circumstances did not in all cases warrant. They joined the historic Irish people—even where in terms of Gaelic descent they had not all belonged to it.[28] A significant number of them promoted the Irish language, spoken as well as written, and it was they who organised the great harp festival of 1793. Because they looked to a future in which the domestic injustice of the present would be corrected, they were free to affirm what was of value in the past and in other people's present. Most importantly, their commitment to extend the bounds of liberty—not just for themselves, but for more disadvantaged people such as Roman Catholics, women and the labourers at home, meant that they could not merely sympathise but actually ranged themselves on the side of the slaves abroad, as we have seen. All this is in marked contrast with the attitudes of the descendants of these same people who, in contemplating the outside world, almost always merely extrapolate from their own situation of threatened dominance in the North of Ireland.

The men and women of the United Irish movement are not, of course, to be idealised. They were not super-people and many of them did not stay the course, but as a movement within Irish history they offer at least one key, which has not often been used to unlock the past and set what is worthwhile in it to work again. In spite of their stature and the magnanimity of their vision, they are generally ignored in twentieth-century Ireland. Revisionist historians tend to circumnavigate them. Dr Conor Cruise O'Brien has taken a different course: he has attempted to discredit republicanism itself by referring to what appears to be inconsistency in the development of Wolfe Tone, the man whom so many look to as the father of Irish republicanism. He sets Wolfe Tone in unfavourable juxtaposition with E.M. Forster as follows: ' "Break the connection', wrote Wolfe Tone "Only connect", wrote E.M. Forster.'[29] But, as Dr O'Brien well knows, the full quotation from Wolfe Tone goes like this:

> To subvert the tyranny of our execrable Government, to break the connection with England, the never-failing of all our political evils, and to assert the independence of my country—these were my objects. To unite the whole people of Ireland, to abolish the memory of all past dissensions, and to substitute the common name of Irishman in place of the denominations of Protestant, Catholic and Dissenter—these were my means.[30]

Tone goes on to say that he despaired of the majority of those who belonged to the Church in which he had himself been baptised, i.e. the Church of Ireland, as by law established:

> Already in possession by an unjust monopoly of the whole power and patronage of the country, it was not to be supposed they would ever concur in measures the certain tendency of which would be to lessen their influence as a party, how much soever the nation might gain.[31]

Tone aimed at substituting the common name of Irishman for that of Protestant, Catholic and Dissenter, and at making the sort of 'connection' between various kinds of Irish people towards which E.M. Forster would in general urge us. When that was done, he knew he must finally break the imperial link, in whose interests the 'past dissensions' and sectarianism had been fostered and maintained, and who is to say that, in the circumstances of the time, Tone was wrong?

But revisionist historians are not alone in depreciating the contribution of the United Irishmen and women. Those of the established political parties who gather each year at Bodenstown at the grave of Wolfe Tone, rarely open his autobiography or other writings. Almost certainly they do not know or seek to know the views of Jemmy Hope or Russell, Mary Ann or Henry Joy McCracken on property or women's rights or on the relations of Church and State—and this for the good reason that, as Peadar O'Donnell put it fairly sharply in the last piece of writing to come from his pen: 'The reality is that the roots of the present regime are not in the independence struggle but in the interests that brought about its defeat.'[32]

It is easy to identify whose garrison the unionists have been made to be over the centuries: the masters of the Dublin establishment of today, on the other hand, are less easy to identify—their addresses are multi-national.

One might expect that the impact of the United Irishmen and women would be felt in West Belfast. But unfortunately this is not really the case.[33] There is probably more than one reason for this: after all, the views of those Dissenters of the last two decades of the eighteenth century were not shared by their descendants within a generation or less of 1798. They melted away. Moreover, the Catholic population of Belfast today descends largely from people who only arrived in Belfast well after the time when the Presbyterians had changed their tune. Their own view of history, insofar as it was orally transmitted, had been conditioned by rural sectarian outrage and later by the sufferings of unskilled Catholic workers hemmed into the miserable streets on every side. Insofar as their view of history was derived from the text-books available in Catholic schools, it was the product of a nationalism which may have saluted the names of McCracken and Tone from the distance, but which was otherwise conditioned to be reluctant to believe that anything of real importance could actually be learned from Protestants. The United Irishmen and women were often at best turned into 'good' Protestants or even into honorary Catholic nationalists. So they were peripheralised. What they had to say about the unholy alliance of priest and king, was conveniently forgotten and its sting drawn. Their potential as a means to re-contextualise the past and open up a more magnanimous future was never exploited.

12

The Role of the Churches—Priestly, Sage-like or Prophetic?

Before turning in the last chapter to the task of sketching tentatively the mode or presence which in future might be expected of the Churches in the fulfilment of their prophetic calling, it may be considered worthwhile to comment on the character of that role (a) in general in the context of present conflicts, and (b) with reference to one particular sensitive area—that of education.

The Role of the Churches in the Northern Conflict

With reference to the role of the Churches in the Northern conflict, the question is often posed as to whether or not the conflict is a religious one. See Introduction, above. In chapters 2 and 3 above, we have already adduced evidence considered relevant to the answering of that question. But just now a number of further points might briefly be made by way of response.

(1) Politics has functioned as a surrogate religion and, more frequently perhaps, religion as a surrogate politics. Two examples, among many which could be cited, may suffice. Pearse's use of imagery drawn from the passion of Christ in order to describe and ennoble the sacrifice he and the Volunteers were about to make has been well-documented and closely studied. But at the same period, when the Ulster unionists were bracing themselves for the coming political struggle, it was upon religious rhetoric that they drew to greatest effect. In 1912 they drew up a 'covenant' which some signed in their own blood. In doing so, they deliberately recalled the *Solemn League and Covenant* of the Scottish Presbyterians of the seventeenth century, behind which in turn lay the covenant of ancient Israel with its God. Cf. what has been said about the appropriation of the history of Israel in chapter 2.

(2) Since 1969 and the early days of the civil rights movement in the North, spokespersons for the Churches have been in two minds as to whether to concede that this is a religious conflict at all. As we have

already seen, the confessional divide has again and again been exploited in Ireland, over a very long period, to divide so that others may rule. Anxious to deflect the accusation that the people of Northern Ireland were still fighting the confessional wars of the seventeenth century, as an outsider might be excused for concluding they were, level-headed leadership in the Churches post-1969 pointed to the economic inequalities, occasionally to discrimination in employment or often to 'interference from Dublin' and the claims to the Northern territory in Articles 2 and 3 of the Irish Constitution of 1937 and other factors as being at the root of the problem. This included some who had, up to then, been hotly denying that there was any religious discrimination—certainly on the side of the border they themselves lived in! In the course of the twenty years since 1969, however, Church people have gradually shown themselves more willing to admit that there is a religious dimension. This view has received a fillip on the Protestant side since two recent referenda in the Republic returned results which it was believed were in line with the thinking of the Roman Catholic Church. Undoubtedly, the results in these referenda came as what one hesitates to call a godsend for unionists, who were able to turn round triumphantly and claim their forebears had been right to chant, 'Home rule is Rome rule!'

(3) We have already alluded to the process whereby, from the seventeenth century on, confessional allegiance was the criterion applied in order to bring about one of the most extensive programmes of expropriation and reappropriation of land to take place in modern European history. But, in all this, we should recall a fact, already adverted to above, in chapter 3, i.e. that there was virtually no indigenous Reformation of the Irish Church. The Protestantism which first robustly and significantly established itself on Irish soil was brought in by outsiders. It was not the dynamic protest and the positive insights of Luther, Zwingli, Bucer or Calvin, but the rigid Calvinist scholasticism of the next century which shouted across the cold hills of Ulster and exchanged abuse with the Catholicism of Trent and the counter-Reformation.[1] Those who locked in conflict in Ireland were two groups, radically and linguistically alien, fighting over the same tracts of land and armed with opposing theologies which scarcely seem at any time to have addressed one another's points.

(4) At a more ecclesiastical and political level it should also be remembered that each of the major religious groupings can be seen by and large to have considered itself what the pioneering German sociologist of religion, Ernst Troeltsch, called a 'Church' rather than what he termed a 'sect'.[2] Troeltsch defined 'Church' as follows:

> A Church is an institution which has been endowed with grace and salvation . . . . it is able to receive the masses and adjust itself to the world, because to some extent, it can ignore the need for subjective holiness, in favour of the objective treasury of grace and redemption.

Clearly his definition would be applicable rather differently in the case of the Roman Catholic Church in Ireland and, say, the Presbyterian Church in Scotland, but it would hold true in both. 'Church' stands, in Troeltsch's definition, in contrast with 'sect'. The latter he defined as 'a voluntary body of believers, living apart from the world and usually excommunicating both society and State.'[2] Irish people born into what may be termed 'Churches' in Troeltsch's definition, have expected the Church to act as the *cultus publicus*, the official religion. Conversely, they have taken it for granted that the State should, as far as possible, reflect the values of the Church. The Church included within itself the widest possible variety of adherents.

In Ireland, however, over the past three to four hundred years, there have been two or three competing national religions—each one with pretensions to be the authentic public cult.

(i) the Roman Catholic Church, the Church of the overwhelming majority at all times has always claimed to be the one holy and apostolic church. Even in the penal times, that claim was still made;
(ii) the Church of Ireland, till 1870 the established Church: by virtue of its established position, it understood itself as a comprehensive settlement, even though it was in a majority nowhere; and
(iii) the Presbyterians who were neither a majority, except for a few areas in the North-East, nor established.

Each of them drew strength and consolation from the thought that they were part of something bigger outside: the title of the established Church till 1870 was, after all, the 'Church of England and Ireland'. The Presbyterians cherished the link with Scotland, which provided for instance the university education they could not get in Ireland itself. By the nineteenth century, Irish Roman Catholicism was beginning to achieve a new self-respect from the rise of ultramontanism.[3] With it came a renewed loyalty to the Holy See whose authority transcended that of the petty kings of earth. This loyalty however, also served to increase the suspicion of Protestants that Roman Catholic loyalty to the State was inherently qualified.

(5) Each of these was able in the seventeenth and eighteenth centuries to carry on more or less as though the others did not exist. By the nineteenth century however, the British government, under the liberal

impulse, sought to hold the ring as the Irish Churches settled down to the effort of dividing Irish life between them into various spheres of influence. Ever since the late eighteenth century there had grown up an increasingly *pragmatic* attitude on the part of Catholic bishops and the British government toward one another. Britain might be Protestant, but at least it was opposed to godless France. As the eighteenth century progressed the bishops found that much could be wrung from the British, who for their part recognised that even though the bishops were Catholic at least they could be relied on not to stir up revolution. From the Church's point of view, the British Empire itself could be seen as providing a sort of infra-structure for Catholic world mission. Home Rule, which the Irish parliamentary party was struggling for, would serve potentially to enhance the position of the Church within the empire. Professor Emmet Larkin it was who first pointed out the irony in the fact that the unexceptionably ultramontane Cardinal Cullen was happy to have the Church of Ireland disestablished without pressing unrealistically for the *establishment* of Catholicism. Consequently he in effect contented himself with one of Pius IX's errors, *Libera Chiesa in libero stato*, though no one was so ill-bred as to point this out—certainly not the British who knew that Cullen's experiences in Rome in 1848 had predisposed him emphatically against revolution.[4] In 1922, there was no establishment of any church. Even in 1937, when the Roman Catholic Church was given a 'special position' in the new constitution, which it had not officially enjoyed under the constitution of the Free State, de Valera drew back from formal establishment. A number of other Churches were 'recognised'.[5]

In 1912, when Home Rule came up for serious consideration in the British parliament for the third time, Irish Protestantism quite simply lost its nerve. They were faced with the possibility of being a minority distanced from the Protestant majority of Great Britain, and came rapidly to the conclusion that it would be best to 'abandon' their co-religionists in three out of four of the provinces of Ireland and even in three of the nine counties of the fourth, in order to be a majority inside a laager. Reluctantly perhaps, one must see this as the betrayal of the Protestant mission and destiny. They were not content to be a mosquito movement, existing not for itself, but for the whole people of God. Over the past eighty years the Protestant Churches have opted to become what may without offense be termed a 'mini-Catholic' group, making the best deal they can for their sectional interests. This is a pity: they could have chosen to use the freedom they might be thought to have as a result of not owing allegiance to the See of Rome, to explore alternative forms of Christian presence.

(6) In the Introduction we noted how three distinct groups of persons are discernible in the life of ancient Israel—the priests, the sages and the prophets. Each of these had a vision of what was most important in the ordering of the nation's life. For the priests it was the temple, the ordering of its sacrifices and hours of prayer at the appropriate time of day and season of the year, that guaranteed the health of the nation. The sages were concerned rather with the study of the Law and its interpretation in the ordering of everyday life. Its prescriptions shedding light on relations between the person who sells and the one who buys, between members of the family, between servants and masters etc. were their constant study. The prophets were certainly not lacking in concern for e.g. the conduct of business or the relations between the rich and the poor, but they were concerned with these things as part of the life of the nation and its destiny. Even the behaviour of the king himself came constantly under their critical scrutiny, as itself being subject to the judgment of God.

Now it would be naïve in the extreme to imagine that we can discover exact parallels in twentieth century Europe or Ireland to these groupings belonging to a Near Eastern country between two and three thousand years ago. Nevertheless, it might not be totally inappropriate to expect to find groups within our contemporary society which, for all the differences between it and ancient Israel, could be said to function for us in a not altogether dissimilar way. To put it differently, we might ask to which of these roles do the Churches in Ireland most commonly approximate? that of sages? that of priests? or that of prophets? In their public interventions, are they concerned primarily with the continuing life of their institutions, their prestige and place in society which might be a contemporary reflex of the priestly role? Or are they primarily concerned with pastoral work, with relations in the family and individuals within a society of which they do not offer, or have no time to offer a critique—which would be a contemporary reflex of the sages' role? Or are they concerned, in their public interventions, to hold the underlying assumptions of economic life, national life etc. up to scrutiny and to express misgivings, even to the point of pronouncing judgment, perhaps even suggesting a better way—which would be a contemporary reflex of the prophetic role?

A full and fair answer to that question would require a major and exhaustive study in itself. At the risk of unfairness and accusations of superficiality we nevertheless select one area in which the Churches are publicly involved and aspects of which have already been touched on above, i.e. education and, in particular, the management and control of schools. This is, after all, an area in which the interests of priests, sages and even prophets may be expected to come into play, or even be in competition with one another.

The reader may feel that there are other areas which would have been a better choice for comment—unemployment, emigration, combating poverty or the Third World. Or s/he may feel that the linked areas of medical ethics and the control of hospitals would be a better ground on which to determine the nature of the Church's role. Certainly, with reference to the last-named sphere, serious questions do arise concerning the Roman Catholic Church's role and a possibly unspoken desire for social control over citizens, particularly over women (a) through its teaching on contraception and the termination of pregnancy, and (b) through its control of the boards of management of hospitals which are largely maintained by state funds. This subject has been widely discussed in the media and in serious academic studies. On that ground alone, it seemed better to concentrate on another area, using at least some material which has not so far been discussed in print.

Before turning to the example chosen, it would be improper not to say something about the role of the Church in combating poverty. No one can fail to be impressed by the extraordinary energy, intelligence and courage of agencies like *Combat Poverty* and others too numerous to name, or the imagination of Bishop Peter Birch of Ossory or the perseverance of Sister Stanislaus Kennedy. The statements of the Churches on poverty, but particularly those of the Roman Catholic bishops and the Conference of Major Religious Superiors and individuals like Sister Stanislaus are as well-documented and as comprehensive as anything produced by the official agencies of the State, and much more hard-hitting. Indeed, they illustrate very clearly the degree to which it is possible and even imperative to live within the sages' vision and the prophets' one, simultaneously. For the CMRS document on poverty, in particular, makes no bones at all about moving from a demand for remedial action to a demand for a restructuring of society and redistribution of wealth, as do a number of the statements which have come from Father McVerry and the Jesuit fathers resident in Summerhill and subsequently in Ballymun. A preoccupation with the relations between people in the flats and between them and the authorities leads to a sharp critique of the ordering of society itself. The 'sages' have become 'prophets'.

The Role of the Churches in education

In seeking an answer to the question about the character of the Churches' role, let us take an example from a well-documented area in which their involvement is a public one—the field of education, and in particular one aspect of the churches' involvement in the schools, north and south, in which their attitudes and behaviour may fairly be compared. The fact that attitudes to a single problem north and south can be compared is itself important.

In his recent magisterial study of the question, Séamus Ó Buachalla has shown the way in which the Minister for Education in the early years of the Free State was reduced to being little more than a cipher.[6] It was to the bishops of the Roman Catholic Church that the government looked for the resources to provide a national system of education and, in return for what they were providing, the bishops could expect as little interference as possible from the State. Into this tacit agreement it was possible to slot the special requirements of the Protestant minority—generally speaking, to the satisfaction of all.

In Northern Ireland in the early years in fairness it should be said that the 1923 Education Act sought seriously to transform education in Northern Ireland by establishing a non-sectarian system combining efficiency with local popular control. But some Protestant clergy with the support of the Orange Order combined to reverse the aims of that Act, as has been admirably documented and described by Professor D.H. Akenson[7] and P. Buckland.[8] The United Education Committee which they formed stated roundly that the 1923 Act opened the door 'for a Bolshevist or an atheist or a Roman Catholic to become a teacher in a Protestant school'.[9] It insisted that religious instruction in schools take the form of Bible instruction, as distinct from the promotion of the tenets of any particular denomination.

This could not be acceptable to Roman Catholics. In the end, with the passing of the Education Act of 1930, Protestant-managed schools were 'transferred' and the Catholic ones became voluntary schools with, it should be said, what was for the time quite generous State support.[10] But in fact, however, the 1930 Act ensured that increasingly the system discriminated in favour of Protestantism. Whereas the 1923 Act had made it illegal to ask about a candidate's religious affiliation in filling a teaching vacancy, the 1930 Act provided that appointments were to be made by regional committees which were to draw 'at least half their members from the transferors of those schools taken over by the regional committees and from among those persons who were formerly managers of any elementary school which had been superseded by a provided school'.[11] By a series of steps, most of them taken in response to Protestant pressure, a dual system had been created on principles not entirely just: the State or 'provided' schools were in effect Protestant schools, now 'transferred', whereas the Catholic children who, in the primary section were disproportionally numerous, were to be educated in schools receiving only half of their building and running costs from the State.

Of the Protestant clergy led by the Rev. William Corkey and the Rev. James Quinn, D.H. Akenson wrote: 'No band of Catholic priests in the former united Ireland had engaged in politics with the energy and efficacy of the Protestant clerics who led the United Education Committee of the Protestant churches.'[12] Meanwhile a meeting of Catholic clerical school managers in the Free State warned in October 1921 at a meeting in Dublin:

> In view of pending changes in Irish education, we wish to reassert the fundamental principle that the only satisfactory system of education for Catholics is one wherein Catholic children are taught in Catholic schools by Catholic teachers under Catholic auspices.[13]

There is no doubt that the authorities in the Department of Education heard this warning and for decades heeded it.

The way in which the Churches north and south have mirrored one another is easily seen with reference to (a) integrated education, and (b) composition of school management boards and Church representation on them.

With reference to integrated education it could be said that, while only a minority of people belonging to either tradition, whether in Northern Ireland or the Republic, are so wholeheartedly in favour of integrated education as actually to campaign for it, attitudes towards integration have tended to vary according to whether a particular confession is in the majority or the minority. It should be said that the Presbyterian Church in Ireland is the only major denomination in Ireland which is on record as being officially in favour. But this is not the same thing as saying that the majority of Presbyterians would agree with the General Assembly's position in practice. Certainly, it would be true to say that in general Protestants regard integration as a good stick north of the border, with which to beat the Roman Catholic Church authorities, while on the whole defending the right of Protestants to 'Protestant education' south and west of it. The Roman Catholic authorities have remained hostile to the idea in both parts of Ireland. Although

Cardinal Cahal Daly may not express himself as robustly as say the late Bishop Neil Farren of Derry on the subject, he nevertheless even in the summer of 1989 is reported to have made difficulties for Catholic parents in Newcastle, Co. Down, in confirmation arrangements of children attending an integrated school there. Anyone who recognises that aside from the Church itself the Catholic school has been for many Catholic people the only institution where cultural values they treasured were ever nurtured and their dignity affirmed, must at least call in question the wisdom of integrated education just yet in Northern Ireland—at least until it is clearer whether the Programme for Mutual Understanding is going to yield any substantial fruit.[14] Cardinal Daly and his colleagues will know best whether it is concern for the immortal souls of the children who attend integrated schools, the protection of Irish culture, language, music, dancing etc., or simply the fear of losing power and control which activates their opposition to integration.

With regard to the composition of school management boards and how the present situation in Northern Ireland was arrived at post-1923, we have already spoken. It may suffice here to draw attention to the curious way in which the attitudes of Church authorities north and south have complemented one another. When Lord Melchett, Minister of State responsible for Education in Northern Ireland set up an official working party under the chairmanship of Professor A.E. Astin in 1977 to undertake a review of the way in which schools in Northern Ireland should be managed, the Protestant Churches who in 1930 had transferred their schools to the State, began to fear for the future of that provision of the 1930 Act which had allowed the 'transferors' a 50 per cent representation on school management boards. They feared, especially in the case of schools which had never been anything but State schools and had never been transferred from any Church or voluntary body whatever, that they would lose 'transferors' rights. Accordingly, they emphasised that the 'transfer' involved much more than mere buildings. So, for instance, the annual report of the State Education Committee of the Presbyterian Church to the 1978 General Assembly stated:

> This [the transfer in 1930] was recognised as the transfer of a whole system of education, in which the Protestant Churches had been involved historically, and not simply the handing over of property or mere 'bricks and mortar'.[15]

One distinguished ecclesiastic at the time even insisted that, when a new housing estate is built and the school opened, we in the Church will 'transfer our children' and therefore should retain our 'transferors' rights as surely as ever before. The speaker had no need of lessons in casuistry. Nor had the Bishop of Ferns, Dr Brendan Comiskey, who shortly afterwards, in 1980, staked out the claim of the Roman Catholic bishops of dioceses within the Republic to mandatory places for their representatives and for representatives of religious orders, notionally rather than substantially associated with them, on the boards of management of the new Community Schools.[16] The sad thing was, of course, that Protestants, whose own representatives had so short a time before insisted on the continuance of transferors' rights north of the border, could scarcely make a credible case against Bishop Comiskey south of it.

The question may now be put as to which of the roles—that of priest, sage or prophet—the Churches, north and south, Catholic and Protestant, adopted in the course of the above narrative. It would be hard to make a case for saying that they ever raised their sights high enough to act prophetically. Certainly, it may be conceded that, north of the border, Catholic authorities have seen that certain values, cultural and religious, were liable to be ignored or misprized if there were no schools in which they could be cherished. Insofar as they have maintained the schools in order to protect those, they should be defended as they fulfil their 'sage-like' function. But we have noted that this can, and arguably has, deteriorated into the exercise of a rather narrow 'priestly' one. In the same way, south of the border, there can be no question but that Protestant Church schools have been maintained by people who felt that certain threatened values could be maintained only within this environment. But we have seen that other interests—largely class interests—cut across the purely religious concerns of the Protestant 'sages', and can be said often to have dominated them.[17]

13

Prophetic Utterance: The Quest for a Model and a Mode of Presence

In chapters 8–10 we explored the meaning of the word *conscience*, finding in it a sense of what we might hesitate to call 'collective conscience', fearing that that has totalitarian overtones, but which might safely be termed 'shared consciousness'. We concluded that it is the duty of Christians, among others, to keep expanding this shared consciousness so as to make it increasingly inclusive. In the Introduction it was noted that the prophets of ancient Israel, often by taking the received wisdom and the inherited narrative of their people and discerning new dimensions and meanings in them, encouraged the people to draw ever wider implications from their commitment to Yahweh. The Christian gospel itself was understood as an ultimate in this process insofar as at its heart lies the conviction that God is calling all through the crucified one without regard to social status, race or sex.

In chapter 7 we recognised the prior importance of developing two other characteristics, which we called *solidarity* and *conformation*. We saw that, in the endeavour to allow God's justice the opportunity to come to expression, everyone is too much involved in present injustice for any to consider themselves qualified to be the dispensers of it. Change, if it is ever to be God's kind of change, can neither be prescribed by the rich nor conceded by the privileged, however benevolent they may be. Of course, the experts, the intellectuals and the privileged must be welcomed in the work for radical change. But they will contribute most constructively when they put themselves entirely at the disposal of the deprived. They will often question the judgment of the poor, the under-privileged or the oppressed, but they must listen and defer to them before they can help them to get themselves up off their knees. Otherwise they are sure to give a faulty diagnosis. Genuine solidarity with the oppressed implies a critique of a believing community which has become no more than a sect, which holds itself aloof from the world and, even when it does involve itself in social work, is committed to doing so strictly within the constraints of its own preconceptions. But it also implies a critique of the believing community which is operating the 'Church model' and which historically has most often sought either to *control* or to *prescribe.*

Conformation is closely connected with solidarity, but there is a difference. Christians have not always recognised that indignation and philanthropy, important as they are, are in the end no more than interim *pledges* of commitment to political action. For political questions require political answers. But the formulation of political agendas is going to mean disagreement and debate, and the implementation of them is necessarily going to involve Christians as readily as anyone else in moral ambiguities of one kind or another. It will involve them on occasion in co-operation and even collusion with those whose motives they suspect.

Dietrich Bonhoeffer, the German pastor-professor who eventually made the decision to become involved in the plot to assassinate Adolf Hitler, himself entered this dark world of ambiguity and learned there a lesson which his Master taught, i.e. that it is not always desirable or even possible to clear one's good name or reputation in the pursuance of this course. In the darkest days of resistance to the Third Reich, Bonhoeffer never tired of making another point which should come to his readers today with as much relief as it did to his students and former students then. He pointed out that ultimate responsibility is not ours. We are not called upon to make final statements or to take the ultimately significant decisions about the Third Reich then or the North of Ireland now.[1]

In the 'interim period', as he called it, between the decisive action of God in Christ, at one end, and the general resurrection at the other, we are called on to exercise whole-hearted obedience by making 'penultimate' decisions. In this interim period we are to be *conformed* at once to Christ and to the world, i.e. conformed to the Christ who was himself conformed to the world in the sense of operating within *all its constraints*, including its ambiguity. In this dual conformation, there is implicit a critique both of the sect model of Christian presence and of the Church model—both of which have at times been deployed by Irish Christians. Those who belong to the sects have opted exclusively for conformation to Christ, and that has really taken them out of the world. Those who opt for the Church model have begun by attempting to comprehend the world within themselves, but have usually ended merely by being 'conformed' to the world. The call today, as ever, is for conformation to the Christ who is conformed so closely to our condition as even to share in its unavoidable ambiguity.

How is shared consciousness to be developed in prophetic speech and action in the Irish situation?

We have already spoken of the excellent and courageous statements produced by the CMRS and the Roman Catholic hierarchy, by the Irish Council of Churches and by other individual Churches on poverty, on political violence, on unemployment and the problems of our emigrants, and a number of other questions. In the production of these statements, the sponsors have taken the most expert advice available to them, so that they cannot easily be faulted on grounds of accuracy. The recommendations have, in many cases, been hard-hitting. These statements are to be welcomed as an eloquent indication that those who produced them are not prepared to allow the Church of the crucified Jesus to be marginalised or to be reduced to the status of a call for the cultivation of individual piety. It is a tacit recognition also perhaps of the claim that the universal call to the whole race through the crucified one is not primarily a call into a religion, but is the divine demand for a new humanity.

Such a claim would probably be perfectly acceptable to three theologians in Germany belonging respectively to Reformed, Lutheran and Roman Catholic traditions, i.e. Jürgen Moltmann, Wolfhart Pannenberg and J.B. Metz.[2] These theologians operate in a country in which the Churches have never been quite disestablished, though it must be conceded that in Germany the process of secularisation is generally speaking considerably more advanced than it is in Ireland. They take the view that Christian Churches are by definition engaged to be participant in the struggle for the transformation of society and the liberation of humankind. Because they are committed to the promise of the kingdom of God, the Churches resist the institutional stabilising of things, and by raising the question of meaning, make things uncertain and keep them moving and elastic in the process of history.

Metz seems sometimes to assume that the social critique he advocates, if pursued sufficiently energetically, is an end in itself which holds the Church together in social engagement, but it is not altogether clear that this is so. Nor can one be altogether clear that, for instance, Moltmann is entirely happy to take up residence in this resting-place. There is, after all, a long Christian tradition, arguably going back beyond Constantine which, while it recognises that here we have no abiding city, nevertheless seeks certain provisional or penultimate norms by which we might at least regulate our social life.

David Hollenbach has referred to a number of extremely thorough theological questions which are being debated within the Church today.[3]

He is talking primarily about the Roman Catholic Church and his experience in North America, but there can be no doubt that what he says applies to other Churches and, with obvious differences, to Churches in Ireland as well.

(i) He notes the extraordinary difficulty, particularly on the part of the Roman Catholic Church, in dealing with any kind of social pluralism. We have already looked at the way the Roman Catholic Church in Ireland was forced by circumstances beyond its control during the nineteenth century to opt for pluralism. At the same time, it minimised the pluralist impact through its educational system and by setting up an impressive system of medical and social care-structures. The recent catastrophic drop in vocations for the religious orders is the main reason but it is not the only one for the breakdown of that system. This breakdown poses serious theological and practical problems.

(ii) There is the problem shared by both Catholics and Protestants in finding a sound basis for the claim to teaching authority outside the realm of doctrinal matters. Knowledge has become increasingly specialised and the faithful know that not even the most intelligent clerics are able to operate in every specialism within which problems arise.

(iii) There are problems about the actual ecclesiastical structures and their adequacy in coping with questions of political or social ethics. The Roman Catholic Church is still hierarchically structured and still has not discovered the secret of how to give actual power even to the various representative bodies set up under the inspiration of the Second Vatican Council—not to speak of the laity in general.

The structures of the Protestant churches in Ireland at first appear to be a good deal more democratic. The General Synod of the Church of Ireland has two lay members for every clergy person, and the General Assembly of the Presbyterian Church is made up of equal numbers of ministers and elders. However, this is not always as good as it looks. First of all, the only lay persons likely to be able to afford to take a week off to attend meetings of Synod, Assembly or the Methodist Conference will tend to be retired, comfortably off, self-employed, or perhaps very occasionally unemployed. The overwhelming majority are middle class which is probably unavoidable, but it is a pity, and repeatedly it shows up in the wording and the underlying prejudices in many of speeches made and the resolutions passed. Secondly, there is a question concerning the appropriateness of the decision-making process itself. The proceedings of General Synod and General Assembly and, to a lesser extent the Methodist Conference, are quasi-parliamentary. Resolutions are brought forward either by Boards of the Synod or Assembly which, like sub-committees of a larger committee, have been working away at the particular question throughout the year, or by individuals. They are seconded and debated and eventually voted upon. Given the basic structure of these assemblies it may be that it could scarcely be otherwise, but it is questionable whether the confrontational parliamentary model is the most appropriate for a Christian assembly. The Society of Friends do not appear to think so.

But the problem certainly arises, once a decision has been arrived at, as to how binding it is upon Church members. Clearly some things are more binding than others. Supposing one of our Churches were to follow the example of the Uniting Church in Australia and delete the *filioque* phrase from the Creed, thus ranging itself alongside the Eastern Church,[4] then presumably that is what ministers and Sunday school teachers would teach—though it is hard to imagine that Church life or worship would undergo a profound change to match the importance of the doctrinal change decided upon. However, when the Presbyterian Church terminated its membership of the World Council of Churches, it did make a difference, because it affected the institution itself and, with a kind of knock-on effect, those members who had represented the Irish Presbyterian Church in the committees and commissions of the WCC.[5] But when the 1988 General Assembly threw out a resolution in favour of sanctions against South Africa and substituted one which called on the Irish and British governments to give aid to the Botha regime, no member of Assembly who believed in mandatory comprehensive sanctions slackened for a moment in their efforts to have such sanctions universally implemented. It is not to be supposed that even those who voted for the resolution of the 1988 General Assembly ever expected that they would! So what really happens in a case like this? The answer is that great efforts are made on the part of proponents of two opposed views, in the interests chiefly of public relations and publicity to get a majority to support the view they hold. When a resolution is passed it means that one group has succeeded and the other, in this very limited forum, has failed to get the 'Church' to give its backing to a cause which that group is already promoting elsewhere and intends to continue to do so, no matter what the 'Church' says.

But if one were to ask which of the two resolutions could command the obedience of members of Assembly and of the Church at large, the answer is of course the one that referred only to the Church itself as institution and its relations with an international body, the WCC. Most other decisions, even if they are on the really important issues e.g.

poverty, war and peace, the nuclear question or racism, are in the realm of exhortations to members or to the world outside from the majority of members of that particular year's General Assembly or Synod.

A peculiar characteristic of the situation of the Churches in Ireland lies in the fact that, the Christian faith up to the present in Ireland has not lost its position as the primary integrative and organising principle for social institutions, as it has in so many other parts of the Western world. Here it is not entirely true even yet, that 'the ultimate and most sublime values have retreated from public life either into the transcendental realm of mystic life or into the brotherliness of direct and personal relations'.[6] Many of us would hope that they never will, but the urgent question is, how can that undesirable retreat be avoided?

Hollenbach describes the situation which he knows best. He says:

> The legitimate autonomy of the political arena, expressed in the principles of religious liberty and separation of Church and State, raises serious questions about the possibility of common Christian action for justice. If common action is to be effective in a bureaucratic society it must be organised action. There is a strong cultural bias present in our society which results in the misrepresentation of any public or political activity by the Church as a violation of the separation of Church and State . . . Cultural pressure to keep the Christian community's action in society non-institutionalised also leads to the fragmentation of Christian efforts to bring greater justice to social organisations. It often leads to the view that religiously motivated actions by individuals are legitimate expressions of religious liberty while such actions by organised groups or Churches are attempts at re-establishment.[7]

The last sentence quoted betrays the difference between the Irish and the American situations. For here in Ireland the Churches have never been wholly disestablished more than in theory, so 're-establishment' cannot be feared. People see the organised action referred to by Hollenbach, not as an effort at re-establishment but as an effort to prevent disestablishment and marginalisation. Against what some would see as the tide of history, governments continue to ask the Churches for their views—perhaps because they cannot think of any other reasonably honest broker they could ask. The questions come, even on matters where technical expertise may be required in order to offer any view at all worth giving. So it is that, even in Northern Ireland, between June 1986 and June 1987 the Churches were asked their view on the following:

Draft order re Reform of Police Complaints and Discipline Procedures;
Draft Order on Fluoridation of Water supplies;

Draft Public Order Northern Ireland Order;
Draft Adoption Northern Ireland Order;
Homeless persons legislation for Northern Ireland.

It would be churlish on their part if they were to refuse to comment and it would be humility beyond what Church people can usually muster to say that they do not know how to respond.

Up to this we have been thinking of the role of national Churches. At the international level we find the world Church, as represented by the Roman Catholic Church or the various organs of the World Council of Churches engaging with all the most serious and challenging questions of our day. Some of their responses, e.g. those of the World Council of Churches through its Programme to Combat Racism, provoked controversy among member Churches, even to the point of contributing to the withdrawal of membership. But no one could say that the WCC has failed to face up to the social, economic and political problems of the time with courage and intelligence. Their awareness and the awareness they have awoken in others deserves to be defended against those who suggest that questions of peace and war, development and the terms of world trade etc. are so complex that they should be left to the experts. Failure of judgment or premature directives on the part of Christian world bodies should not lead us to conclude that specific action on the great social political and economic questions are not our business at all.

In response to the perceived danger of allowing Christian faith to retire into the realm of the mystical and the private, there has been initiated a quest for an agreed set of principles derived from the synthesis of theological and social analysis of this or that issue. No doubt this quest runs certain risks; the theological and the social are sometimes merely juxtaposed, rather than synthesised. But they are being kept together, and that is the important thing. But where the case for the defence of the WCC has been heard, it must be admitted that there is something to be said for the criticism which Paul Ramsey directed against the report of the WCC Conference on Church and Society of 1966.[8] Ramsey contends that the conference had often quite misunderstood the nature of political decision-making and had in any case, assumed in itself an expertise it quite simply did not have. He is quite clear that Christian commitment does not give those who have it particular political skills. One suspects, however, that Ramsey would be very happy if Christian Churches and groups would leave questions concerning economics, the terms of world trade or, in 1966, Vietnam to one side and let others get on with it.

He does, however, offer a valuable distinction in corporate Christian action between what he calls 'directions' of a more general kind and 'directives', which call for a quite specific line of action in a particular situation.[9] For the first he sees plenty of scope while for the second he sees only very occasional opportunities.

Ramsey does prompt a question as to whether or not there is in the Churches today a dangerous tendency towards justification by works, which expresses itself in the desire to pronounce on everything or be seen to be involved everywhere? Is there a danger in bodies like the WCC or the world confessional bodies coming to see themselves increasingly in 'papalist' terms? They see the Pope going everywhere and talking about everything, and they want to do the same. Instead of limiting themselves to statements which make certain general points, lay down certain general guidelines, set out the terms of certain constraints inside which Christians believe this or that question must be worked at, these bodies, or important people within them, seem to hope to 'bind' their membership to a position of considerable specificity, as though their credibility as Christians depended on their adherence to that particular line.

One suspects that this premature specificity arises fundamentally from the desire to walk by sight where we can walk only by faith. Perhaps it is of the nature of the Christian way that most often when we meet together we can agree only on *directions*, not on an agreed list of *directives*. Then, in a rather fragmented way, we must go back to the world in separate and one hopes perhaps mutually respectful groups to work on the problem in our own way. As we work away in our separate groups, sometimes taking mutually exclusive lines, on South Africa or the future of Northern Ireland or whatever, we have to work out our obedience in faith not sight. In doing so we will not ask to be backed up by a legislative majority in any court, secular or ecclesiastical, nor will we excommunicate those who working with the same Christian constraints arrive at different conclusions. We have to consider that *small groups in disagreement* is sometimes the only form the Church Catholic, in social action, can take today. We will not necessarily have the satisfaction of being sure at every moment that our little group really is the Church in action at all. But while that is very disturbing and even frightening, we must simply go on to 'sin boldly' recognising that 'the Church' which the Creed speaks of is an item of *faith*.

Whatever, under Christ, we do in the end pluck up courage to say or do, one thing is certain. Anything *worthwhile* in our corporate social action will be shaped, not alone by the masterly character of our social or theological analysis, but by the coming glory.

The sun behind the cloud on a spring day in Ireland sends out shafts of light to different groups at different angles. As the wind blows the cloud, the lights and shadows race over the fields, up the hill and over the sea, farther than we can follow. The sun from which we draw our light is so much greater than our vision that we will catch its rays in a thousand different ways. With hands shaken from a realisation of the fragility of all human obedience and perseverance, we may, however, take the perspective glass into our grasp. We may just catch a glimpse of what is to come and 'some of the glory of it', and then set off again.

Notes

Introduction (pp. 1–9)

1. J. Neusner, *Judaism in the beginning of Christianity*, London 1984, 38. See chapter 2, 'Three types of Judaism in the age of Jesus: sage, priest and messiah,' 35–44.
2. E. Troeltsch, *The Social Teaching of the Christian Churches*, 2 vols. ET. London 1931.
3. Isaiah 6 and Jeremiah 7.
4. Luke 12:54–56/Matthew 16:2–3.
5. K. Koch, *The Prophets, Volume 1, The Assyrian Period*, ET. London 1982, 5.
6. Amos 9, 7–8.
7. Koch, *The Prophets*, 6.
8. Koch, *The Prophets*, 4.
9. 2 Samuel 12:1–15.
10. E. Troeltsch, *Social Teaching*, ii 321.

Chapter 1. Winners' and Losers' Stories (pp. 10–17)

1. Deuteronomy 26:1–11, Cf. Deuteronomy 6:20–25.
2. A.D. Falconer (ed.), *Reconciling Memories*, Dublin 1988.
3. C. O'Brien, *States of Ireland*, London 1972.
4. J.M. Coetzee, *Waiting for the Barbarians*, London 1984.
5. J.M. Coetzee, *Waiting for the Barbarians*, 154.
6. J.M. Coetzee, *Waiting for the Barbarians*, 155–6.

Chapter 2. The Function of the Story: (1) Protestant-Unionist (pp. 18–30)

1. See chapter 1, note 1 above.
2. See G. Von Rad, *Old Testament Theology*, Vol II, trans. D.M. Stalker, Edinburgh/London 1963.
3. *Tuatha* (plural) is the word used for the tribal groupings of early Ireland, of which there were between 150 and 200 in the early christian period.

4. E. MacNéill, *Celtic Ireland*, Dublin 1921, chapter 3.
5. V. Crapanzano, *Waiting, The Whites of South Africa*, New York 1986, 68.
6. *Reports to the General Assembly of the Presbyterian Church in Ireland*, Belfast 1987, 179.
7. V. Crapanzano, *Waiting, The Whites of South Africa*, 61–2.
8. A. Buckley, 'The Chosen Few, Biblical Texts in the regalia of an Ulster Secret Society' in *Folk Life* 24 (1986–6), 5–24.
9. A. Buckley, 'Walls within walls: religion and rough behaviour in an Ulster community' in *Sociology* 18/1 (Feb. 1984), 19–22.
10. J.W. de Gruchy, *The Church Struggle in South Africa*, London, 2nd ed. 1986, 31.
11. The Synod of Dort (1618–19) was convened to settle differences within the Reformed Church in the Low Countries over the doctrine of predestination and atonement. Its conclusions can be summarised under five headings: (1) the assertion of the total depravity of human nature, (2) a belief in the unconditional election of individuals, (3) belief in 'limited' atonement, i.e. the conviction that Christ died only for the elect, (4) belief in the irresistible character of God's grace, i.e. that God effects what God wills, and (5) a belief in the perseverance of the saints, i.e. the conviction that those whom God elects will not defect from their calling but will 'confirm' it.
12. For an account of the 'subscription controversy', see J.L.M. Haire et al., *Challenge and Controversy, Essays in Irish Presbyterian History and Doctrine*, Antrim 19881, 96–133.
13. A.A. Fulton, *J. Ernest Davey*, Belfast 1970.
14. W. Gibson, *The Year of Grace*, Edinburgh 1860.
15. I. Nelson, *The Year of Delusion*, 1862.
16. F. Holmes, *Henry Cooke*, Belfast/Ottawa 1981, 189.
17. In a paper delivered to the annual meeting of the British Association for the Advancement of Science 1986, Section 1–19, 12–13.
18. A. Buckley, ibid. 1986, 13.

Chapter 3. The Function of the Story: (2) Catholic-Nationalist (3) The 'Protestant Nation' (4) The 1916 Proclamation (pp. 31–39)

1. I.C. Smith, *The Exiles*, Dublin 1984, 36, quoted by A. Falconer in *Northern Ireland, a Challenge to Theology*, Edinburgh 1987, 32.
2. See Alan Falconer (ed.), *Reconciling Memories*, Dublin 1988.
3. H.M. and N.K. Chadwick, *The Growth of Literature*, Cambridge (1940) 1986, I. 304ff., II. 544, 695ff., III. 143, 398ff., 601ff., 814ff.

4. J. Bannerman, *Studies in the History of Dalraida*, Edinburgh 1974.
5. D. McCartney in F.X. Martin and F.J. Byrne, *The Scholar Revolutionary*, Shannon 1973, 95.
6. See below, chapter 11.
7. *Belfast City Plan*: 1988 submissions were invited from organisations and individuals on all aspects of municipal life.
8. In chapter entitled 'Bards, beasts and men' in D. Ó Corráin, L. Breatnach and K. McCone (eds.) *Sages, Saints and Storytellers, Celtic Studies in honour of Professor James Carney*, Maynooth 1989 (Maynooth Monographs 2), 102–21.
9. L. de Paor, *The Peoples of Ireland*, Indiana 1986, 191.
10. Charles O'Conor (1710–91) of Belanagare, Irish antiquary. See article in *DNB* xiv 855b–857a, reprint 1959–60.
11. James Macpherson, *Fragments of Ancient Poetry collected in the Highlands of Scotland, and translated from the Gaelic or Erse Language*, Edinburgh 1760.
12. The bibliography is enormous, but the following should be mentioned: D.S. Thomson, *The Gaelic sources of Macpherson's Ossian*, Edinburgh and London: Oliver and Boyd 1952. See also F.J. Stafford, *The Sublime Savage* a study of *James Macpherson and the Poems of Ossian*, Edinburgh 1988.
13. This was Adam Ferguson, whose father had been minister of the parish of Logierait in Perthshire.
14. Linda Spencer, *'Wilderness' and 'Civilisation' in eighteenth-century Scotland and America*, unpublished M.Litt. thesis, Aberdeen University 1973–4.
15. Dr Hugh Blair, *A Critical Dissertation on the Poems of Ossian*, London 1763, 13.
16. For significant differences between Scottish and Irish usage of the words *Gaeltacht* and *Galltacht*, see D. Ó Corráin, L. Breatnach and K McCone, *Sages Saints and Storytellers*, 106–8.
17. This identification came to a climax in the publications associated with the celebrations in 1932 of Patrick's arrival in Ireland, particularly in the writings of W.S. Ker.
18. The foundation of the Gaelic League was largely the work of Dr Douglas Hyde, the son of a Church of Ireland clergyman, rector of Frenchpark, Co. Roscommon. See Dominic Daly, *The Young Douglas Hyde*, Dublin 1974.
19. L. de Paor, *Peoples of Ireland*, 208.
20. See Martin and Byrne, *The Scholar Revolutionary*, passim.

21. P. Mac Aonghusa and Liam ó Réagáin, (eds.), *The Best of Tone*, Cork 1972. Seán Cronin, *Irish Nationalism, a history of its roots and ideology*, Dublin 1980, 40–64.
22. I take the points made by contributors to E. Hobsbawn and Ranger, (eds.), *The Invention of Tradition*, Cambridge 1983.

Chapter 4. Stories with/without an End in View (pp. 40–55)

1. P. Lehmann, *The Transfiguration of Politics*, London 1975, 7.
2. P. Lehmann, *The Transfiguration of Politics*, 9.
3. P. Lehmann, *The Transfiguration of Politics*, 6.
4. J. Sachs, 1990 Reith Lectures, six lectures on 'The persistence of Faith', publ. *The Listener*, 15, 22, 29 Nov, 6, 13 Dec 1990, 3 January 1991.
5. E. Moloney and A. Pollak, *Paisley*, Swords 402ff.
6. On William McGrath, see Moloney and Pollak, *Paisley*, 242–3, 282–6, 344.
7. V. Crapanzano, *Waiting, The Whites of South Africa*, 30, tells of a preacher from the Free State who identifies SWAPO as the Anti-christ—'It's hard to accept the fact of the birth of the Antichrist, but you can't dismiss it offhand. It may well be true.' In chapter 13 Crapanzano describes the Renewal movement in some detail.
8. The Rev. J.B. Armour was Presbyterian minister of Trinity Church, Ballymoney, Co. Antrim from 1869 till the end of his life. He was a Home Ruler, but his letters during the first World War, in particular, show his loyalty to the British Empire.
   See J.R.B. McMinn, *Against the Tide, a calendar of the papers of Rev. J.B. Armour, Irish Presbyterian minister and Home Ruler 1869–1914*, Belfast 1985.
9. Calton Younger, *Arthur Griffith*, Dublin 1981. This view they shared with intelligent unionists like the writer of an article in the *Irish Review* who signed himself as 'An Ulster Imperialist' to an article entitled 'Nationalism and Imperialism' in *The Irish Review*, Vol. 1 (March 1911—Feb. 1912) 63–71.
10. A. Warner, (ed.). *The Selected John Hewitt*, Dundonald 1981, 41–3.
11. A. Warner (ed.). *The Selected John Hewitt*, 54.
12. A. Warner (ed.). *The Selected John Hewitt*, 15.
13. V. Crapanzano, *Waiting, The Whites of South Africa*, 26.
14. Quoted Denis Worrall in *English-speaking South Africa Today*, Oxford 1976, 196.
15. V. Crapanzano, *Waiting, The Whites of South Africa*, 35.
16. C.C. O'Brien, *States of Ireland*, London 1972.

17. Hanna Arendt, quoted by Lehmann, *The Transfiguration of Politics*, 6.
18. Frantz Fanon, *A Dying Colonialism*, trans. Haakon Chevalier with foreward by G.M. Carstairs, London 1970.

Chapter 5. Identifying the Enemy (pp. 56–66)

1. The Programme for Mutual Understanding is a secondary school project set up in Northern Ireland in 1989.
2. See chapter 3 note 1 above.
3. P. Levi, *If not now, when*? Translated from the Italian by William Weaver, London 1986, 54–5.
4. The Provisional IRA came into being officially in January 1970. It was formed in protest against the demilitarisation of the IRA during the sixties which left the Catholics streets unprotected in August 1969. Desmond Greaves, *The Irish Crisis*, London 1972. L. de Paor, *Divided Ulster*, London 1965.
5. (a) James Connolly, August 1914: 'This war appears to me as the most fearful crime of the centuries. In it the working class are to be sacrificed that a small clique of rulers and armament makers may sate their lust for power and their greed for wealth. Nations are to be obliterated, progress stopped, and international hatreds erected into deities to be worshipped.' Quoted by Ruth Dudley Edwards, *James Connolly (Gill's Irish Lives)*, Dublin 1981, 120. His Citizen Army marched under the motto: 'Neither King nor Kaiser, but Ireland.' (b) John Maclean, 1915: 'We do not think national wars are of benefit to the workers, so we shall oppose all national wars as we oppose this one. The only war that is worth waging is the Class War, the workers against the world exploiters, until we have obtained industrial freedom.' Quoted by Nan Milton, *John Maclean*, London 1973, 97. (c) Karl Liebknecht in March 1916 delivered a speech in the Reichstag in which he alleged that German soldiers had been killed by guns sold by the German arms manufacturer, Krupps, to Belgium. A fortnight later, he called on the soldiers in the trenches and workers at home to turn upon their common enemies, the land-owners and proprietors. On the following May Day he issued a manifesto to this effect, was arrested and condemned to thirty months penal servitude. See Milton, *John Maclean*, 130.
6. These phrases are Wolfe Tone's. See P. MacAonghusa and Ó Réagáin, *The Best of Tone*, passim.
7. *Minutes of the General Assembly*, 1956.
8. *The Irish Times*, 3 August 1988.

9. D. Bonhoeffer, *Ethics*, ed. E. Bethge, ET London (3rd impression 1978) 55.
10. Cf. Hebrews 9:24–10:18 where the distinction is drawn between permanent radical cleansing and mere temporary relief.
11. The question of how/if crimes against humanity should be punished was raised very sharply by the Nürnberg Tribunal's proceedings. It is arising again now with reference to the eventual fate of the members of the South African regime, but it can scarcely be held to be relevant to the subject matter of this book.

Chapter 6. Expiation in Christian Perspective (pp. 67–71)

1. W.R. Rodgers, *Collected Poems, with an introductory memoir by Dan Davin*, London 1971, 133.
2. 'Epitaph on a tyrant' in *W.H. Auden, Collected Poems*, ed. Edward Mendelson, London 1976, 149.

Chapter 7. Solidarity and the Problem of Identifying (pp. 72–78)

1. Edward Norman, *Christianity and the World Order (BBC Reith Lectures, 1978)* Oxford, 1979, 23.
2. Dr Cahal B. Daly, Bishop of Down and Connor, now Cardinal Archbishop of Armagh, has been one of the Joint Chairmen of the Joint Group on Social Questions, authorised and instituted by the Irish hierarchy of the Roman Catholic Church and the Irish Council of Churches. The role he played as a member of the hierarchy's delegation to the Forum has been widely appreciated.
3. E. Norman, *Christianity and the World Order*, 5–6.
4. The People's Democracy were a militant group of (mostly young) people who emerged in the early days of the civil rights movement in Northern Ireland in 1969; their fundamental orientation was Trotskyist.

Chapter 8. Informing Conscience (pp. 79–86)

1. *Marriage, the Family and Divorce*, 1986. A referendum was held in the Republic in June 1986 to decide whether the article in the Constitution (article 42.3.2) prohibiting divorce should be removed.
2. *The Irish Times*, 12 June 1986.
3. Quoted T. Inglis, *Moral Monopoly, The Catholic Church in Modern Irish Society*, Dublin 1987, 87.
4. *The Irish Times*, 10 February 1984. Tom Inglis, *Moral Monopoly*, 78, speaks of the bishops as 'strategically vacillating' between the

requirement that Catholics adhere to the Church's teaching as regards social legislation and the position that it is a matter which each individual decides in full consideration of the issues and their implications.

5. *The Irish Times*, 10 February 1984.
6. *The Irish Times*, 10 February 1984.
7. *The Irish Times*, 10 February 1984.
8. T. Inglis, *Moral Monopoly*, 70.

Chapter 9. Conscience as Consciousness of the Other (pp. 87– 102)

1. C.A. Pierce, *Conscience in the New Testament*, London 1955.
2. The purpose of the meeting, held in 1972, was to persuade the IRA to end their bombing campaign.
3. J. Miranda, *Being and the Messiah, the message of St John*, trans. John Eagleson, New York 1977.
4. There was 'power-sharing' Executive in Northern Ireland during the years 1971–1974.
5. PSEC: The Protestant Secondary Education Committee, set up to administer the block grant given annually by the government to the Protestant secondary schools in the State.
6. Controversy vis-à-vis VEC Colleges and their management, 1980.
7. One notable example of this would be the vision behind the foundation of the Irish Christian Brothers. See Desmond Rushe, *Edmund Rice: the Man and his Times.* Dublin 1981.
8. Miranda, *Being and the Messiah*, 37.
9. Miranda, *Being and the Messiah*, 37.
10. ed. Austin Flannery, *Vatican Council II: the conciliar and post-conciliar documents*, Dublin 1975.
11. Note the sequence in Romans 6.1ff.
12. Alasdair Heron, *Two Churches—one Love: interchurch marriage between Protestants and Roman Catholics*, Dublin 1977.
13. *Pour la communion des Églises, L'apport du Groupe des Dombes 1937–1987*, Paris 1988, para. 8. English translation by Pamela Gaughan, *Towards a Common Eucharistic Faith, Argument between Roman Catholics and Protestants*, London 1973.

Chapter 10. Conscience as Awareness of the Imminent and Creative Function of the Future (pp. 103–114)

1. Margaret Mead, *Culture and Commitment, a study of the generation gap*, London 1970.

2. *The Irish Times*, 13 July 1986.
3. Mead, *Culture and Commitment*, 3.
4. Mead, *Culture and Commitment*, 34–5.
5. Mead, *Culture and Commitment*, 61.
6. Mead, *Culture and Commitment*, 61.
7. Mead, *Culture and Commitment*, 90.
8. Mead, *Culture and Commitment*, 83.
9. Mead, *Culture and Commitment*, 90.
10. ed. John M. Carroll, and Lance A. Millar *Talking Minds: The study of language in cognitive science*, Cambridge Mass. 1984.
11. *The Pope in Ireland: addresses and homilies*, Dublin 1979, especially 76–82.
12. This is in fact the title of a book about the Marcan community by H.C. Kee—*The Community of the New Age: studies in Mark's Gospel*, London 1977.
    Cf. E. Käsemann's seminal essay, 'On the subject of primitive Christian Apocalyptic' in *New Testament Questions of Today*, London 1969, 108–137.
13. See below, chapter 13, p. 147.
14. J.C. Beker, *Paul the Apostle. The Triumph of God in Life and Thought*, Edinburgh 1980, 155.

Chapter 11. Recovering a Past which the Future can Use (pp. 115–129)

1. See chapter 4, note 1 above.
2. E.P. Sanders, *Paul, the Law and the Jewish People*, London 1983.
   J.C. Beker, *Paul the Apostle*, 235–254.
3. Romans 9–11.
4. R.L. McCartney QC, A Northern Ireland barrister, has been the most forceful poponent of the idea that Northern Ireland should be integrated completely with Britain and, in particular, that the British political parties should be encouraged to campaign in Northern Ireland.
5. Ireland is not the only member of the EC to have a colonial past. Belgium gained its independence from the Netherlands in 1831. The greater part of modern Greece gained independence from the Ottoman Empire in 1832, but the process of regaining Greek territories in the mainland and in the islands continued right up to 1948.
6. See G. Fitzgerald, *All in a Life, an Autobiography*, Dublin 1991.
7. See R.B. Mc Dowell, *Irish Public Opinion 1750–1800*, London 1944.

R.B. Mc Dowell and D.A. Webb, *Trinity College, Dublin 1592–1952* with a foreword by F.S.L. Lyons, Cambridge 1982.
Joseph Liechty's forthcoming study of Irish evangelicalism subjects a number of them to detailed study.

8. The Royal Academy was founded in 1785–6.
9. Edmund Burke (1729–97) was born in Ireland and educated at Trinity College. He went to England as a young man. See *DNB* III, 345a–365a. His controversy with Thomas Paine over the French Revolution was closely followed in Ireland.
10. R.B. Mc Dowell, 'The Volunteers and the Irish Revolution of 1782', chapter IV of *Irish Public Opinion*, 51–73.
11. Thomas Paine, *Rights of Man*, edited with an introduction by Henry Collins, London 1969, reprinted 1971, 1976.
12. On H.J. and M.A. McCracken, see *Mary McNeill, the Life and Times of Mary Ann McCracken, A Belfast Panorama 1770–1866*, Dublin 1960.
13. Seán Cronin, *Jemmy Hope: A Man of the People*, Dublin 1964. R.R. Madden, *Antrim and Down in '98*, Dublin: n.d.
14. M. McNeill, *Mary Ann McCracken*, 145.
15. Genesis 45:24.
16. Madden, *Antrim and Down in '98*, 108.
17. Madden, *Antrim and Down in '98*, 92.
18. Madden, *Antrim and Down in '98*, 98.
19. From the McCracken Letters in Madden Papers, T.C.D. quoted M. McNeill, *Mary Ann McCracken*, 177.
20. McCracken letter, quoted M. McNeill, Mary Ann McCracken, 294.
21. M. McNeill, *Mary Ann McCracken*, 127.
22. *The Shorter Catechism*: Q.7: What are the decrees of God? A. The decrees of God are his eternal purpose, according to the counsel of his will, whereby, for his own glory, he hath foreordained whatsoever comes to pass.
23. M. McNeill, *Mary Ann McCracken*, 290.
24. Madden, *Antrim and Down in '98*, 149.
25. Madden, *Antrim and Down in '98*, 149.
26. The Regium Donum was a grant first paid by William III to ministers of the Synod of Ulster in appreciation for their loyalty.
27. This sentence lists some Presbyterian perceptions; it does not imply that they were all well-founded. For instance, it is arguable that O'Connell was, in point of historical fact, essentially an Enlightenment figure. Certainly he was an ally of Bentham and an opponent

of slavery. He asserted that, in campaigning for Catholic emancipation, he was seeking nothing for Irish Catholics which should not be conceded equally readily to the Protestants of Italy and Spain.

28. As witness the surnames of many of them: Teeling, Emmet, Hope, Kilburn, Russell.
29. C.C. O'Brien, *Neighbours, The Ewart-Biggs Memorial Lectures 1978–1979*, London and Boston 1980, 33.
30. *The Autobiography of Wolfe Tone 1763–1798*, edited with an introduction by R. Barry O'Brien, London vol. 1, 50–51.
31. *The Autobiography of Wolfe Tone* , 51.
32. O'Donnell, Peadar, *Not yet Emmet: a wreath on the grave of Seán Murray*, Dublin 1985, 15.
33. Speeches of Sinn Féin leaders over the past two decades rarely, if ever, quote from their recorded words.

Chapter 12. The Role of the Churches—Priestly, Sage-like or Prophetic? (pp. 130–139)

1. See B. Fitzpatrick, *Seventeenth-century Ireland: The War of Religions*, New Gill History of Ireland 3, Dublin 1988.
   See M.P. Maxwell, 'Strafford, the Ulster-Scots and the Covenanters' in *Irish Historical Studies* XVIII/72 (Sept. 1973), 524–51.
2. E. Troeltsch, op. cit. Introduction note 10 above.
3. See D. Bowen, *Paul Cardinal Cullen*, Dublin 1983.
4. See E. Larkin, *The Roman Catholic Church and the Creation of the Modern Irish State, 1879–1886*, Dublin 1975.
5. *Bunreacht na hÉireann (Constitution of Ireland)*, Baile Atha Cliath (Dublin) 1937, art. 44.2. The clause according a 'special place' to the Roman Catholic Church was deleted by referendum in 1978.
6. See S. Ó Buachalla, *Educational Policy in Twentieth-Century Ireland*, Dublin 1988.
7. D.H. Akenson, *Education and Enmity: The control of schooling in Northern Ireland, 1920–1950*, New York 1973.
8. See P. Buckland, *The Factory of Grievances, Devolved Government in Northern Ireland, 1921–39*, Dublin 1979.
9. P. Buckland, *The Factory of Grievances*, 253.
10. P. Buckland, *The Factory of Grievances*, 262–3.
11. P. Buckland, *The Factory of Grievances*, 263.
12. P. Buckland, *The Factory of Grievances*, 247.
13. P. Buckland, *The Factory of Grievances*, 249.
14. Already referred to in chapter 5 note 1 above.

15. General Assembly of the Presbyterian Church in Ireland, Annual Reports 1978, Belfast 1978, 193.
16. *The Irish Times*, 31 August 1980.
17. See chapter 9 above.

Chapter 13. Prophetic Utterance: The Quest for a Model and a Mode of Presence (pp. 140–148)

1. See D. Bonhoeffer, *Ethics*, ed. E. Bethge, ET, London 1963, 55.
2. See J. Moltmann, *Theology of Hope: on the ground and implications of a Christian eschatology*, trans. J. Leitch, 1969. J. Moltmann, *The Experiment Hope*, trans. M.D. Micks, London 1975. W. Pannenberg, *Ethics*, trans. K. Crim, London 1981. J.B. Metz, *Faith in History and Society, toward a practical fundamental theology*, trans. D. Smith, London 1980. J.B. Metz, *The Emergent Church, the future of Christianity in a post-bourgeois world*, trans. P. Mann, London 1981.
3. D. Hollenbach, 'A Prophetic Church and the Catholic Sacramental Imagination' in J.C. Haughey S.J. (ed.) *The Faith that does Justice, examining the Christian sources for social change*, 234–63.
4. The *filioque* clause in the Nicene Creed states that the Spirit proceeds from the Father *and the Son* (filioque).
5. This decision was taken by the General Assembly in 1985.
6. Quoted by D. Hollenbach, 'A Prophetic Church, etc.' in J.C. Haughey, *The Faith that does Justice*, 236.
7. D. Hollenbach, 'A Prophetic Church,' in J.C. Haughey, *The Faith that does Justice*, 237.
8. P. Ramsey, *Who speaks for the Church? A Critique of the 1966 General Conference on Church and Society*, Edinburgh 1969.
9. P. Ramsey, *Who speaks for the Church?*, 57.

Index